MINERAL SPIRITS

A WHIMSICAL VOYAGE INTO CRYSTAL MAGIC

VOLUME 01

CREATED BY CARRIE A. WEAVER

ISBN: 979-8-9868184-2-9

Printed in the United States of America.

Cover design by Carrie A. Weaver

Interior design by Carrie A. Weaver

Original Watercolor Illustrations by Carrie A. Weaver

DEDICATION

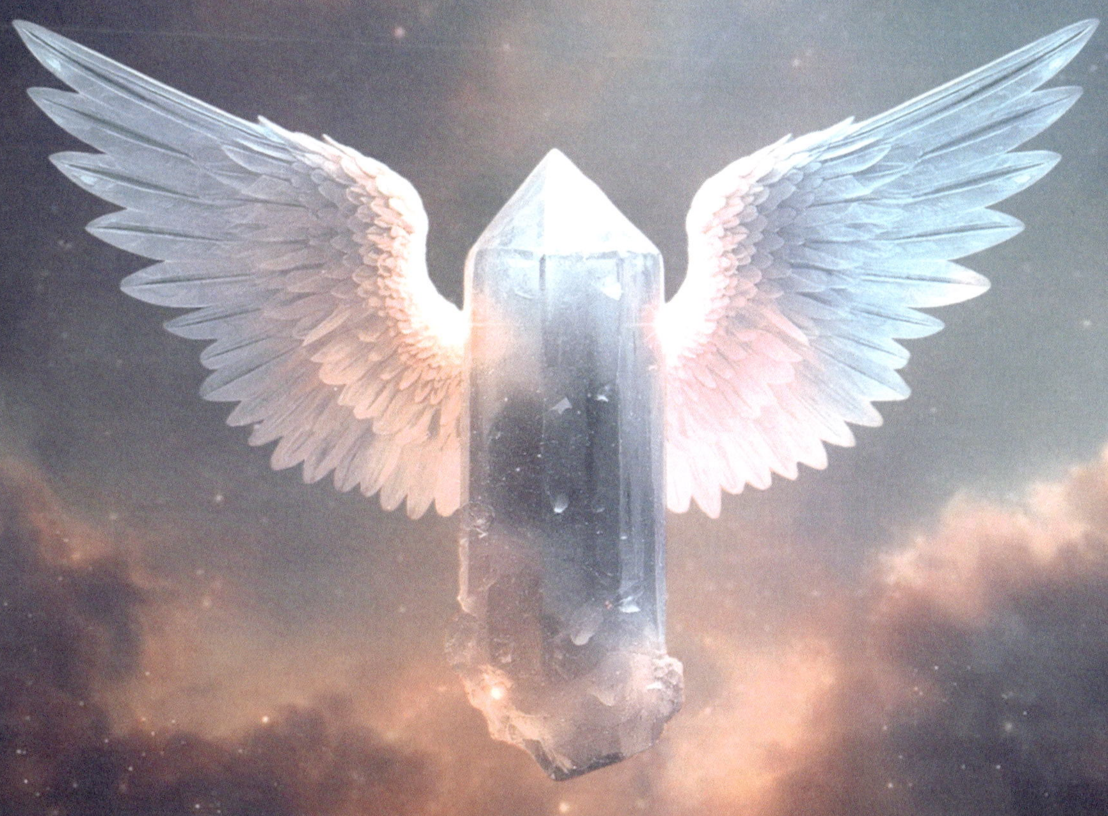

To my teachers, mentors, coaches, and guides...

Your investment in me has changed my life in ways you may never realize.

I am because of you.

INTRODUCTION

Welcome to *Mineral Spirits,* a journey that celebrates the intersection of art, science, and spirituality through the enchanting world of minerals. In these pages, you will discover my original watercolor illustrations, each bringing to life the stunning hues and unique forms of sixteen mineral spirits. The background images were generated using artificial intelligence in Canva. The mineral spirit personas were written by yours truly. The overall design, including the cover, interior layout, and visuals, was created by me, Carrie A. Weaver. I outsourced nothing and feel so dang proud. These mineral spirits each embody powerful and playful metaphysical personas, offering insights and inspiration. As you explore this collection, immerse yourself in an experience that transcends mere observation; expect to feel, reflect, and connect. Whether you're a seasoned mineral/crystal enthusiast, an art lover, or simply curious about the inorganic structures of the natural world, *Mineral Spirits* invites you to engage your senses and awaken your inner wisdom. That's what it did for me. Speaking of which...

For me, *Mineral Spirits* was the gift I didn't know I needed. Creating this art project became a vehicle for my inner wisdom to surface, for my creativity to be expressed, and it allowed for the time to sit in acceptance and generate self-love.

My sincere hope is that the vibrant energies of these mineral spirits delight you and then illuminate your path of personal growth.

Mineral Spirits was born of love.

Please pass a copy forward in love.

GETTING STARTED

After reading *Mineral Spirits,* you'll be so delighted and energized to acquire the cast of characters that you might be tempted to buy your mineral samples online. Here's what I recommend:

- **Support your local gem and mineral store**. Shopping at your local store or at a regional rock and mineral show not only supports your community but also lets you see and touch the samples. When buying minerals, you have to let them speak to you - touch and hold a few samples to see which ones feel like they belong with you before purchasing. Energy doesn't lie.

- **Lab-created samples are just okay**. While lab-created samples have the same chemical properties and crystalline structure as the earth-created versions, they may not have been born with the same universal intelligence as the naturally occurring stuff. Have caution when buying low-cost samples online for this reason. Lab-created samples don't have the same pizazz.

- **Start or deepen a meditative practice**. There are several wonderful meditation apps. Two of my favorites are Insight Timer and Sam Harris' *Waking Up*. Calming the mind by sitting in participation with the present moment is one of the oldest and most impactful practices for enhancing self-awareness, self-acceptance, and, ultimately, self-love - all beneficial things.

- **Share your journey with others**. We live in a time when genuine connection can help heal the collective pain in the world. If you're worried about others thinking your interest in crystals is too "woo-woo," who cares? The world needs your empathy & love, and that change starts from within. If YOU feel better and can spread more love as a result of your exploration with *Mineral Spirits*, then mission accomplished. Not everything has to be so serious. Just have fun with it.

MEET THE MINERAL SPIRITS

09: Kunzite "Kozi" 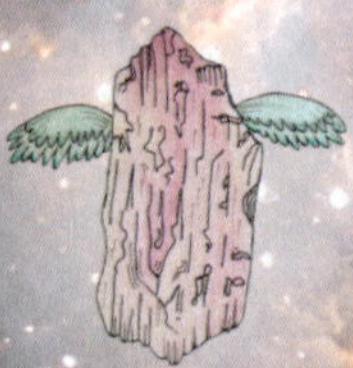

17: Black Tourmaline "Term" 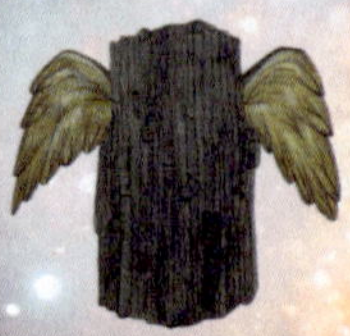

10: Aragonite "Rag" 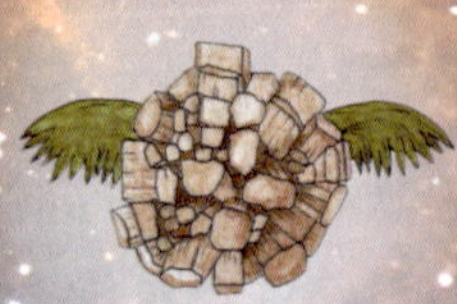

18: "Dolly" Garnet 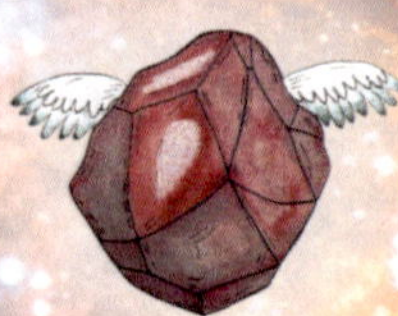

13: Kyanite "Kai" 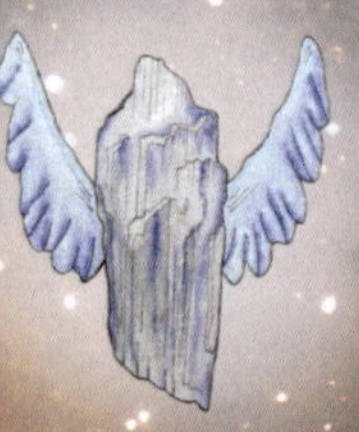

21: Malachite "Mal" 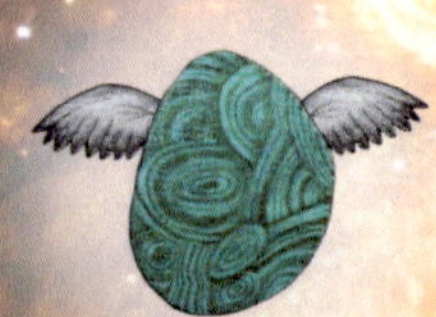

14: Magnesite "Mags" 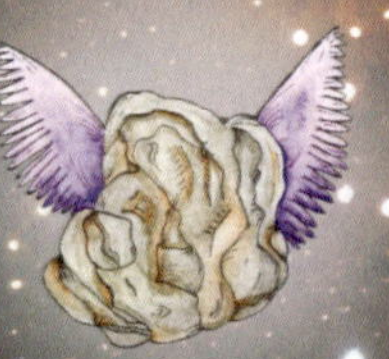

22: Amethyst "Thistle" 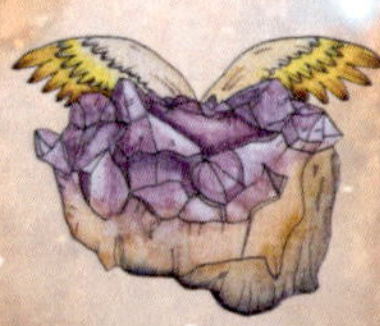

CAST OF CHARACTERS

25: Epidote "Epi" 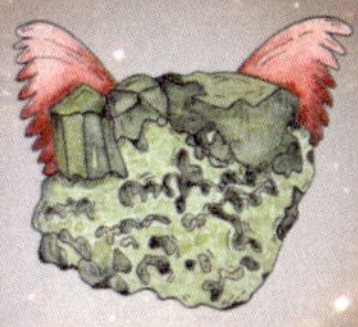

33: Green Calcite "Cal" 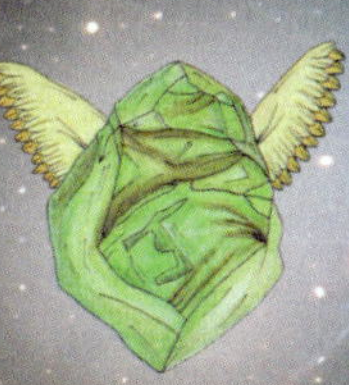

26: Chrysocolla "Chrys" 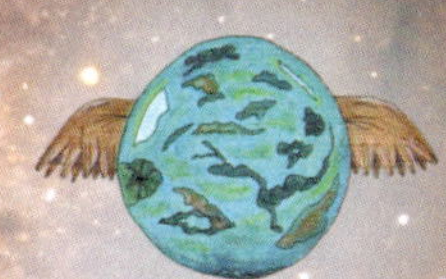

34: Bismuth "Busy" 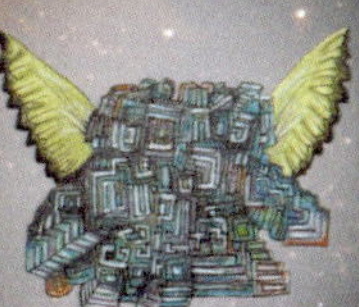

29: Red Agate "Aggie" 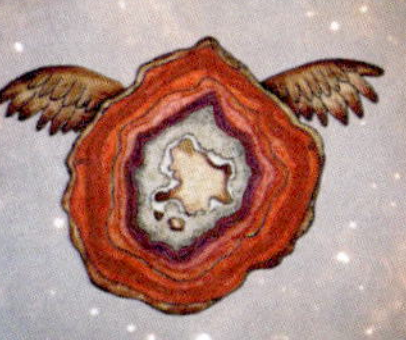

37: Celestite "Celine" 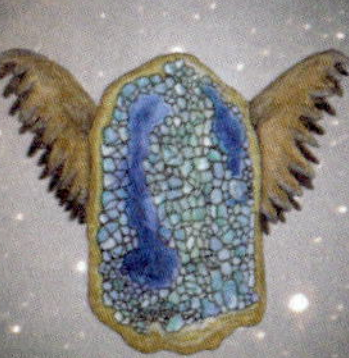

30: Scolecite "Luce" 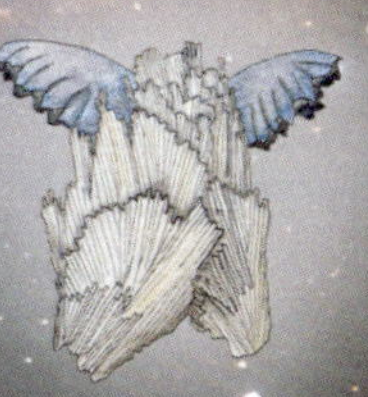

38: Lemurian Quartz "Lem" 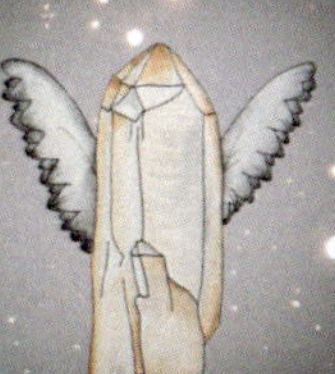

"Let Love Shine In" - Kozi

Meet *Kozi Kunzite*, the love bug of the mineralverse. This pink beauty is the cosmic hug you didn't know you needed. Her core objective is to open your heart and watch it grow a few sizes. With every flap of her wings, Kozi fills your aura with gentle, loving energy, making you feel like you've just gotten a fuzzy, shiny present inside your cells. Working on your self-love game? Kozi's got you, boo. She's weathered all emotional storms and knows how to boost your self-acceptance, helping you forgive, forget, and maybe even giggle at that awkward moment in your past. She's here to remind you that life is too short not to sparkle. Embrace Kozi's tender power and glow like the star you are, bright, beautiful, and ready to spread love like a glitter confetti bomb.

Kunzite *aka Kozi*

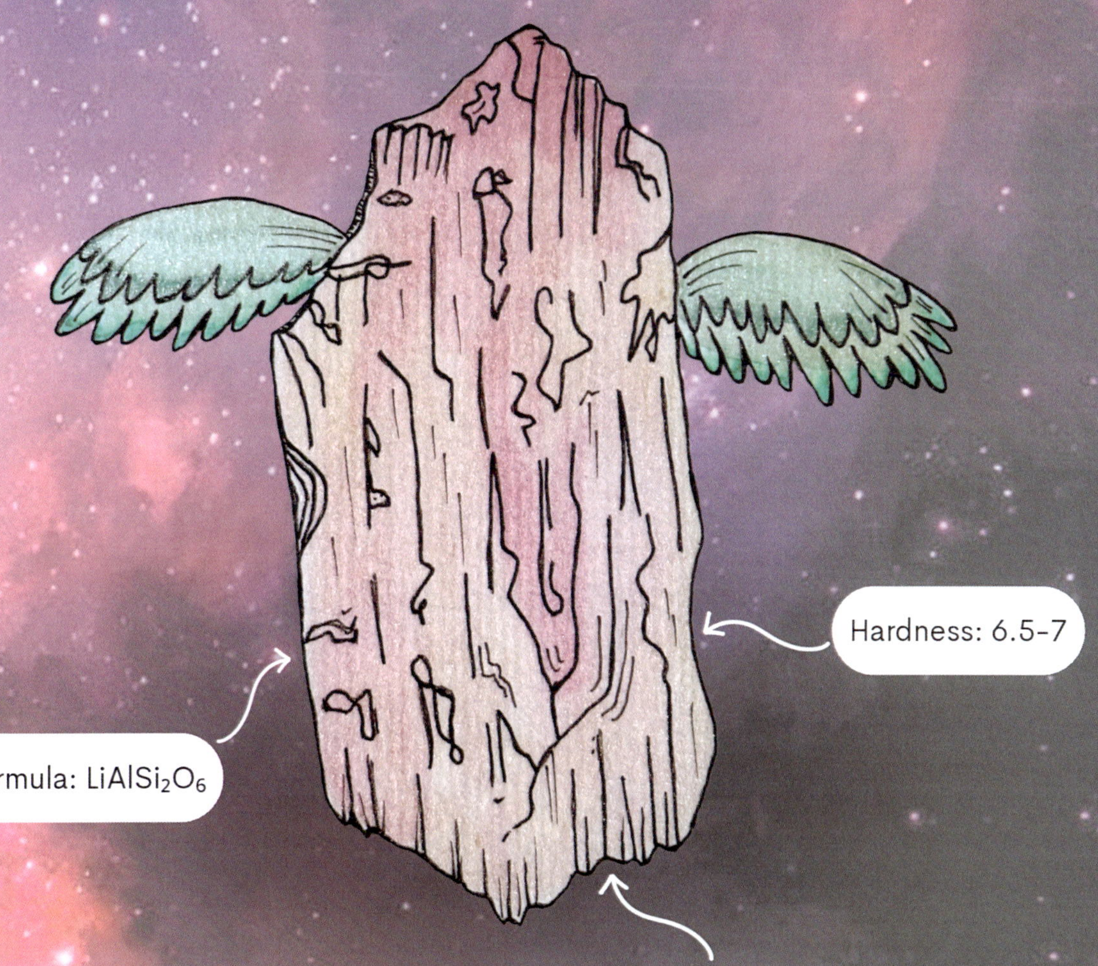

ARAGONITE *aka Rag*

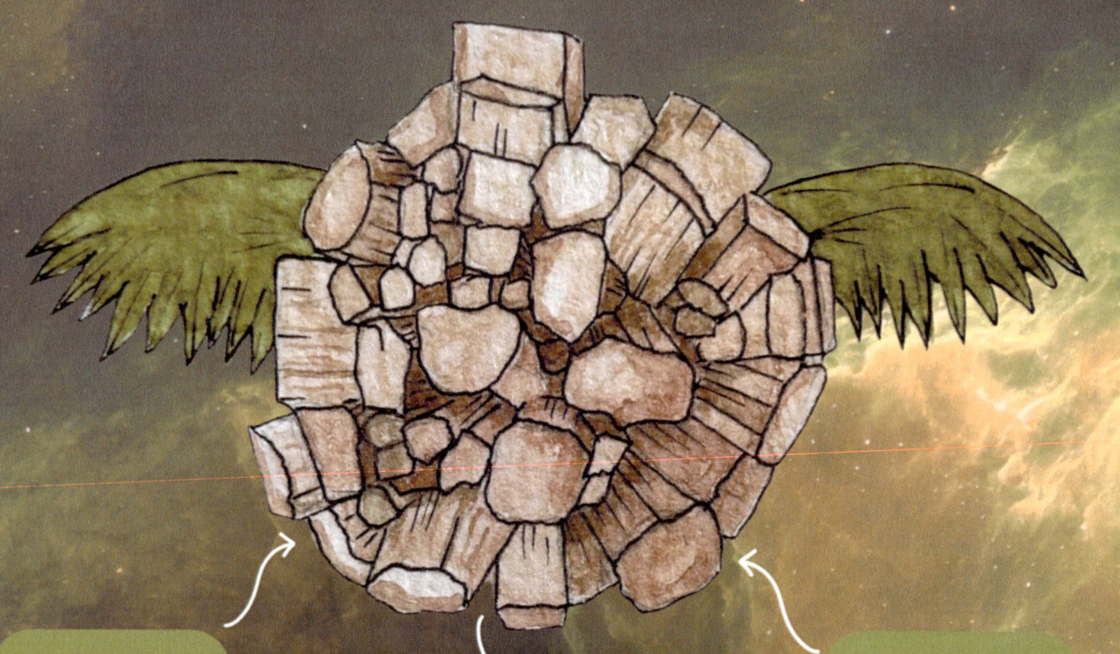

"ROUND YOUR EDGES" - *Rag.*

Here comes Aragonite, aka *Rag*. She's your personal life coach in crystal form. This earthy gal is like having a cheerleader that whispers, "You've got this," every time life hands you lemons. Known for her ability to bring balance and harmony, Rag is like a spa day for your soul, minus the cucumber slices. She's your mineral spirit guide when the chaos of life reaches diva-level drama and your inner zen is out to lunch. Got scattered thoughts? Rag will sweep them up like a psychic vacuum cleaner, leaving room for clarity, peace, and the occasional epiphany about life's mysteries. And let's be honest, who doesn't need a little help with that? Embrace Rag's grounded vibes and let her "round your edges."

"SPEAK YOUR TRUTH" - Kai

Welcome, *Kyanite Kai*, the crystal equivalent of a cool breeze on a hot day. Kyanite is seriously smooth and refreshingly honest. This striking blue guy cuts through confusion and clears the way for clear communication. Kai helps you say what you mean without stepping on toes or losing your cool. He'll instantly align your throat chakra, allowing you to speak as if you were on a truth serum, but with kindness and respect. Kai is your ultimate wingman, encouraging you to stand tall, with courage and grace. When you want to keep it classy yet fierce, keep Kai by your side and enjoy the clarity, calm, and witty comebacks that flow. Always remember: Kai is your guy supporting you to "speak your truth."

Kyanite *aka Kai*

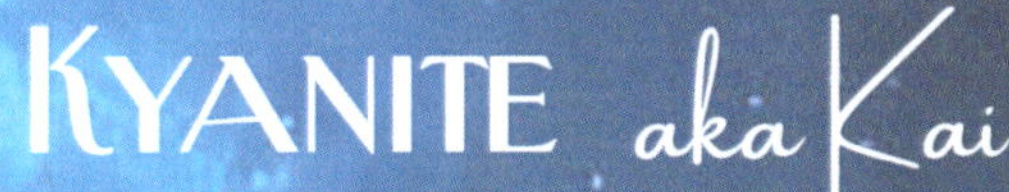

MAGNESITE *aka Mags*

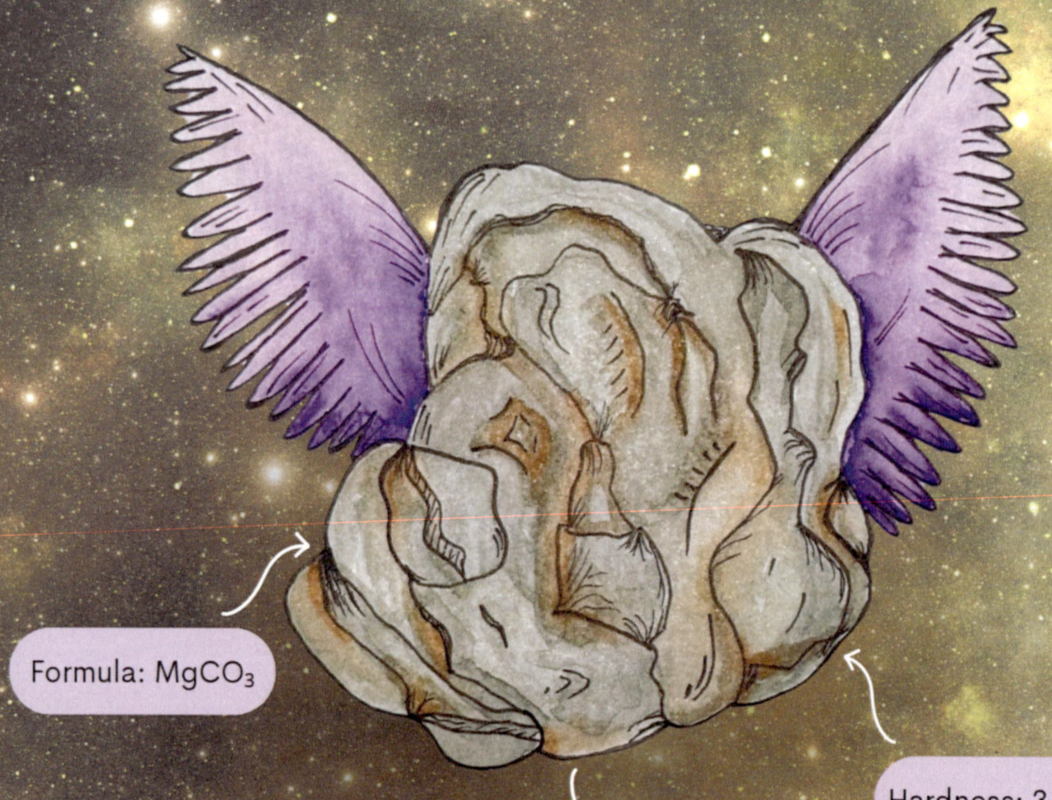

Say hello to *Magnesite Mags*. This mighty mineral is your secret weapon against stress and agitation, acting as your personal mental masseuse. Mags helps smooth out anxiety and keeps your energy on a chill setting; think of her as duct tape for your frayed nerves. She'll nurture your self-love and shepherd you towards living your "one wild and precious life." She keeps you moving forward one step at a time, even when things feel bleak. When life gets overwhelming, Mags is your BFF who reminds you to breathe, relax, and stay in the present moment. No other spirit friend does serenity quite like a bit of magnesium magic. Mags always comes to the rescue, reminding you to "quiet the mind."

"SLAY ENERGY VAMPIRES" - *Term*

Meet Black Tourmaline, a.k.a *Term*, the bouncer of the mineral realm. This dazzling dark knight isn't in it for the glitz and glamour; he's all about protection. Known for his ability to soak up negativity like a sponge, Term is your go-to buddy when life becomes a tad much. Whether shielding you from bad vibes or soaking up the emotional trash left by your work frenemy, this mineral marvel is like a negativity detox in a black-tie package. Plus, he'll ground you faster than a text from your mom after midnight. Oh, and let's not forget his flex—he's got abs stronger than steel. So, next time life throws shade, grab *Term* and blast through negativity like a laser cannon. Whether times are good or bad, he's got your back. Term is your mineral spirit guide when you need to "slay energy vampires."

BLACK TOURMALINE *aka Term*

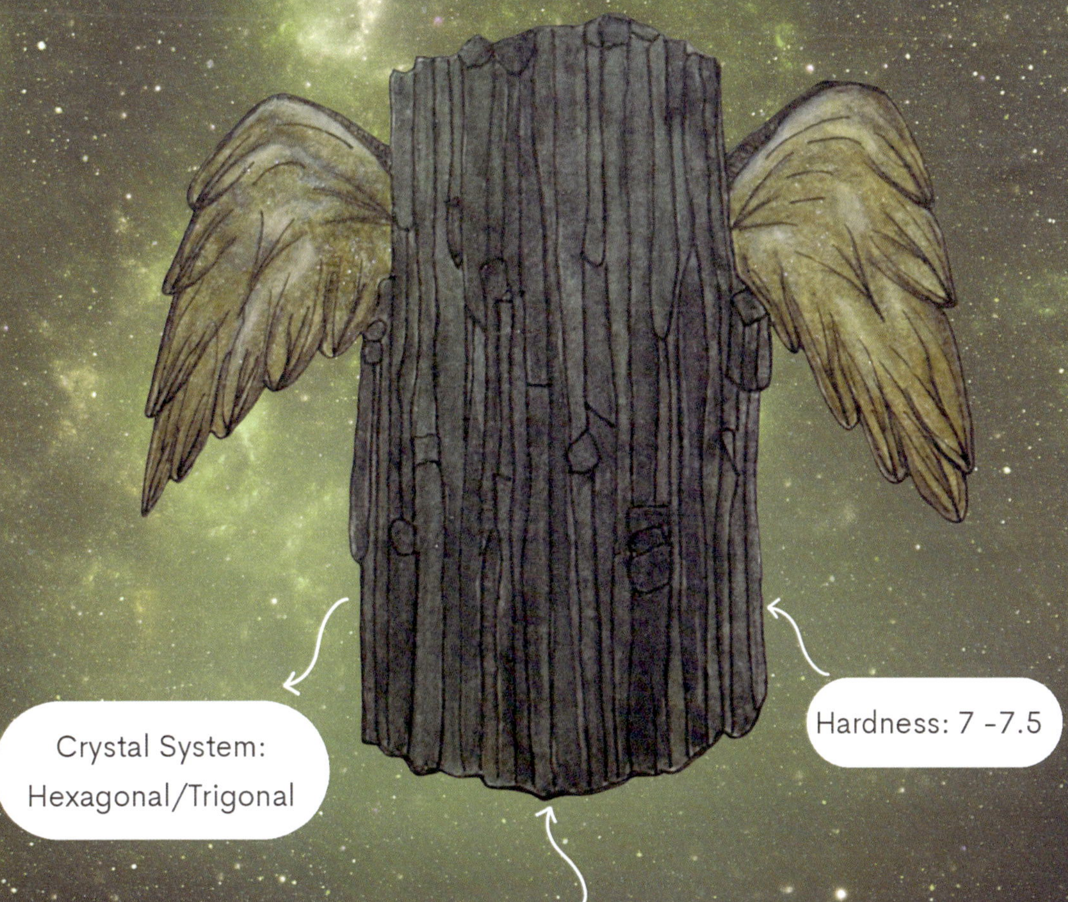

Garnet aka Dolly 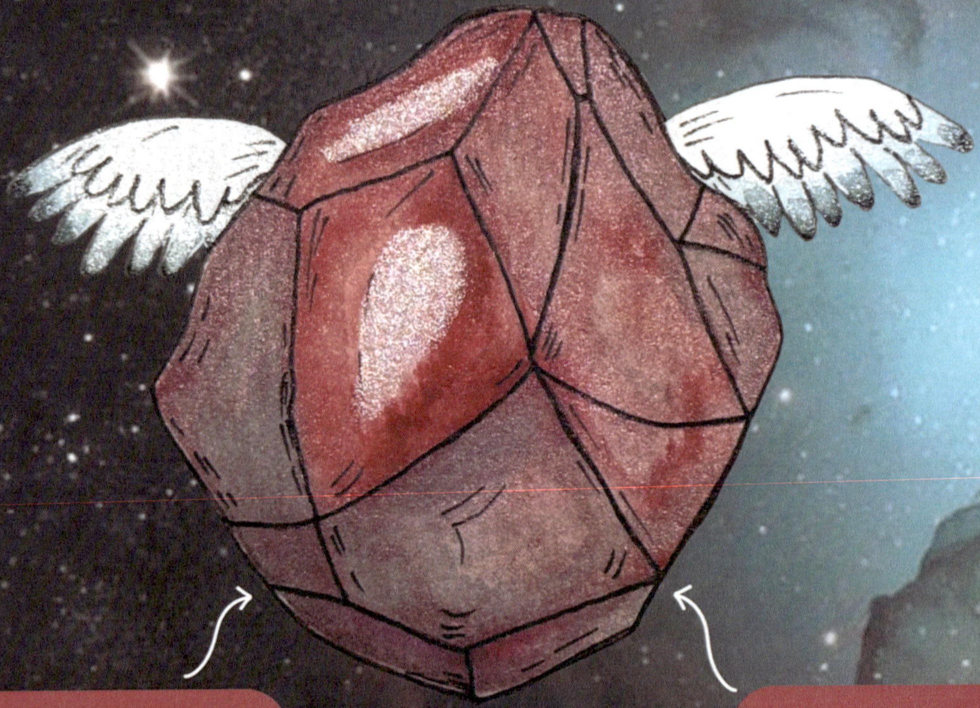
Formula: $Fe^{2+}_3Al_2Si_3O_{12}$
Hardness: 6.5 - 7.5
Crystal System:
Isometric/Dodecahedral

"Ignite Your Fire" - Dolly

Meet *Dolly Garnet*. This deep, fiery jewel of the Almandine variety isn't just here to impress with her perfect crystal structure; she's your creative compass and energizer, wrapped into one. Dolly will infuse you with a fiery sense of purpose, igniting your ambition while reminding you that you're capable of conquering anything – from mundane Monday meetings to life's big adventures. Known for boosting vitality and drive, Dolly will keep your energy levels higher than your bank account balance, and she helps with that, too. She's got a side hustle as an ultimate protector who fights off fatigue and negativity. Allow Dolly to help you "ignite your fire," because with this crystal by your side, you're basically a walking, talking empowerment rally—loud, proud, and totally fabulous, just like Dolly.

"GET DOWN TO BUSINESS" -Mal

Greetings, *Malachite Mal*! This green guy is a catalyst for meaningful change. Mal's striking banded patterns are meant to evoke confidence while inspiring you to become your best self. Mal encourages you to face your shadows and take honest steps toward transformation, turning uncertainty into a source of strength. He's the mineral spirit that helps you "get down to business." With clarity and focus, he'll inspire you to dissolve old barriers and open the door to new possibilities. You can't ignore the rich green hues whispering beyond the crystalline structure, telling you that profound change starts from within. With Mal as your spirit pal, you'll find the courage to embrace growth, face challenges head-on, and make the shifts you need to move forward. Carry or wear Mal as a reminder that transformation is a process—sometimes quiet, sometimes messy, sometimes powerful, and always worth it. So are you.

MALACHITE *aka Mal*

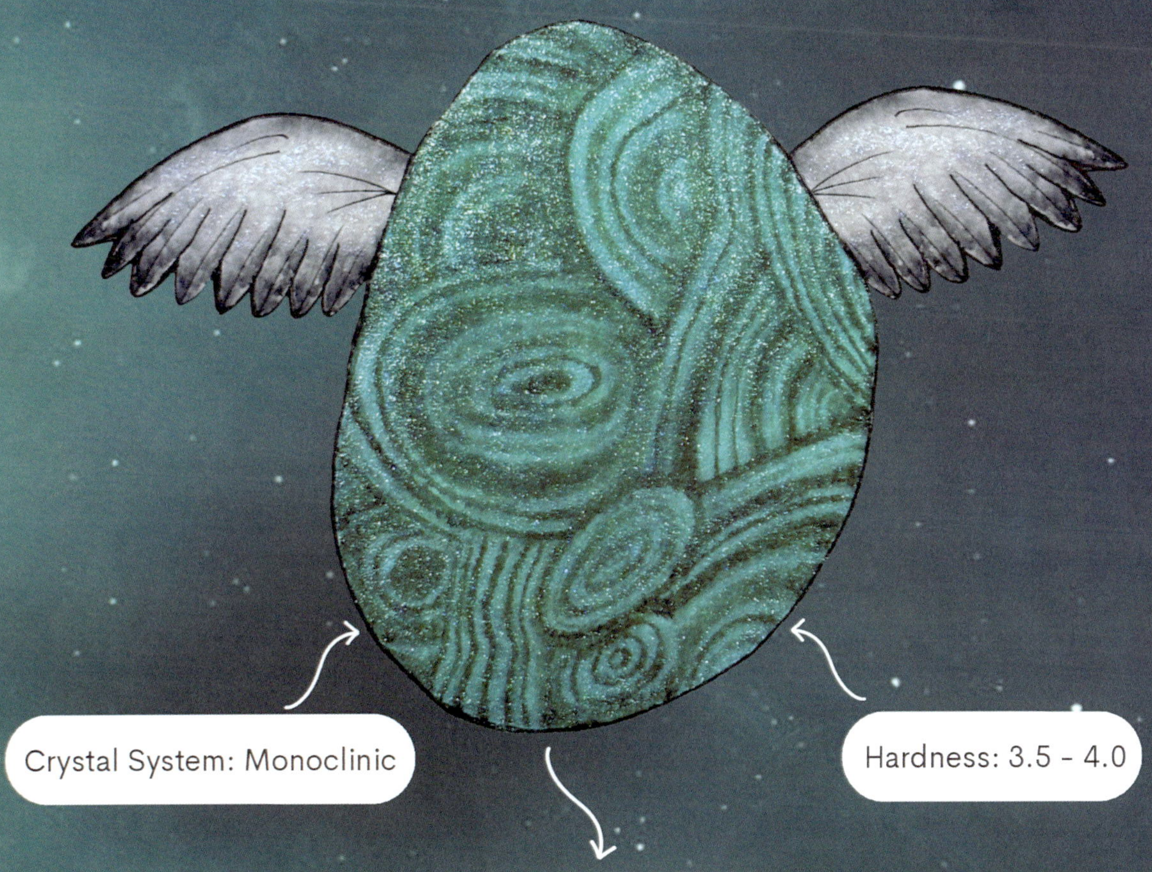

AMETHYST *aka Thistle*

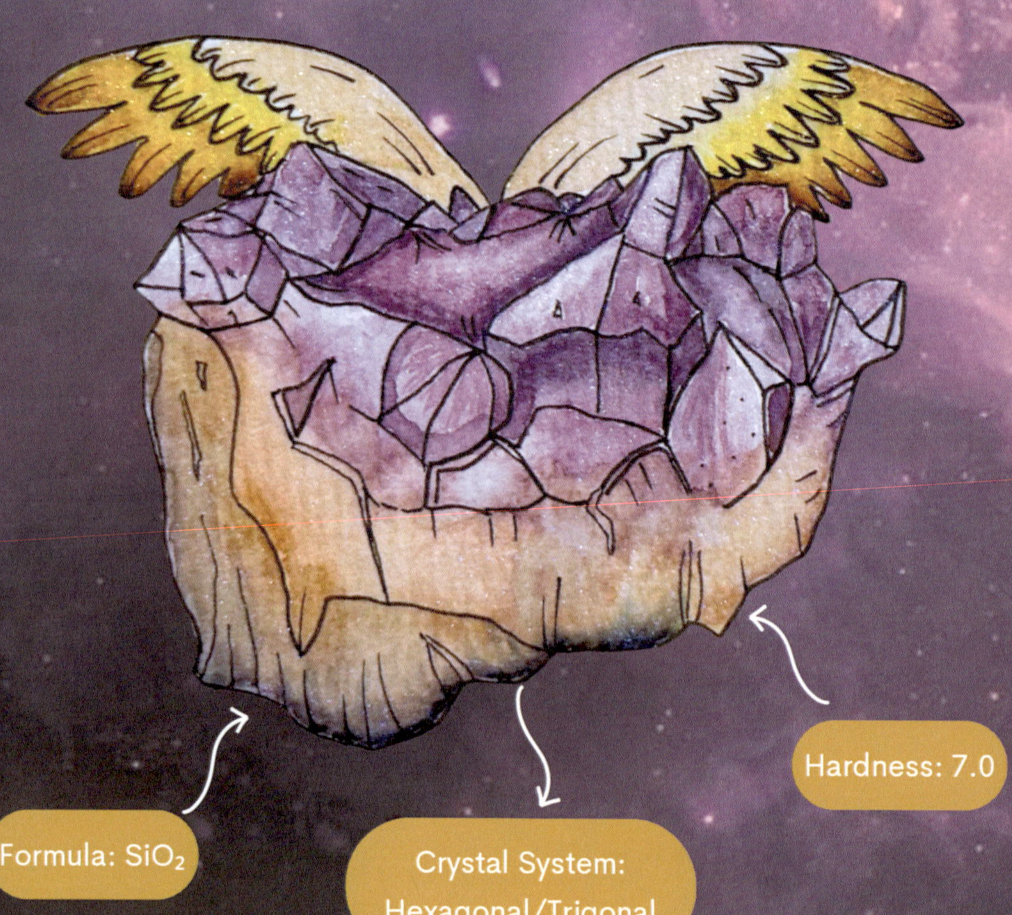

"Live Your Purpose" - *Thistle*

Hello Purple Pal, Amethyst, aka *Thistle*. Violet is in style for anyone needing to dial up living in alignment with their greatest purpose. Known for her ability to sharpen intuition, Thistle will help you see through the muck of life and find a spiritual needle in a cosmic-sized haystack. She's your wise sage insisting you take a moment to breathe and get your head straight. With her rich purple hues, Thistle reminds you that true peace starts from within. There's no need to search outside yourself; just a little crystal magic will do. Carry Thistle when life gets noisy, and begin to feel the flow of inner wisdom as your new default setting. Because when your mind is clear, the world is your oyster and you're meant to be the pearl.

"Grow Beyond Limits" —Epi

Why hello there, *Epidote Epi*. They give sparkle in the shadows. Don't put this green-black beauty in a box. They're more than a pretty face; they're your secret weapon for transformation with a touch of mischief. Epi is known for clearing roadblocks while stimulating growth. They act like a backstage pass to your personal evolution. Is there really a way to stay grounded while reaching for new heights? Yup. That's Epi. Think of them as your inner gardener, pruning negativity and cultivating resilience. This mineral spirit energizes your zest for life by upgrading your mental models. Need a little push to shake things up? Epi will be there to lend a wing. They're your confident and slightly rebellious sidekick that says, "grow, baby, grow," with a push but also a parachute. Embrace Epi's magic and get ready to "grow beyond limits," because they're here to turn potential into pure, dazzling proof.

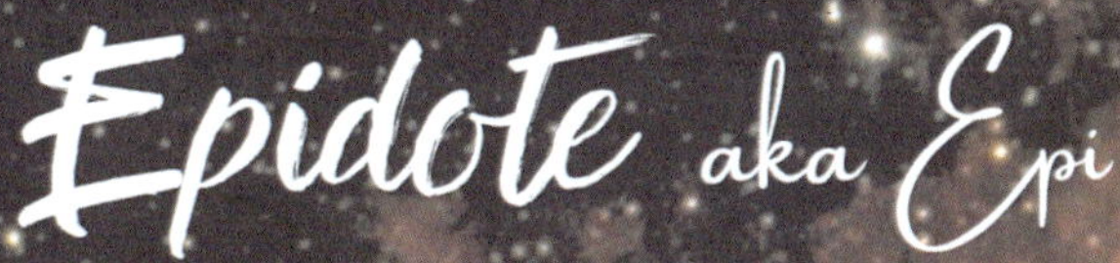

Epidote aka Epi

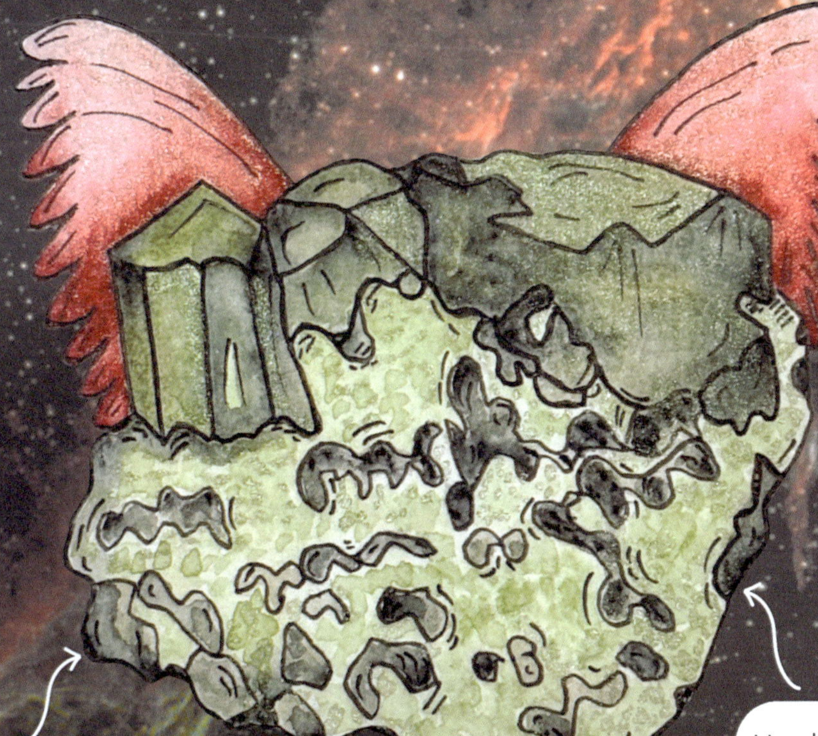

Crystal System: Monoclinic
Hardness: 6 - 7
Formula: $Ca_2(Al,Fe)_3Si_3O_{12}(OH)$

CHRYSOCOLLA *aka Chrys*

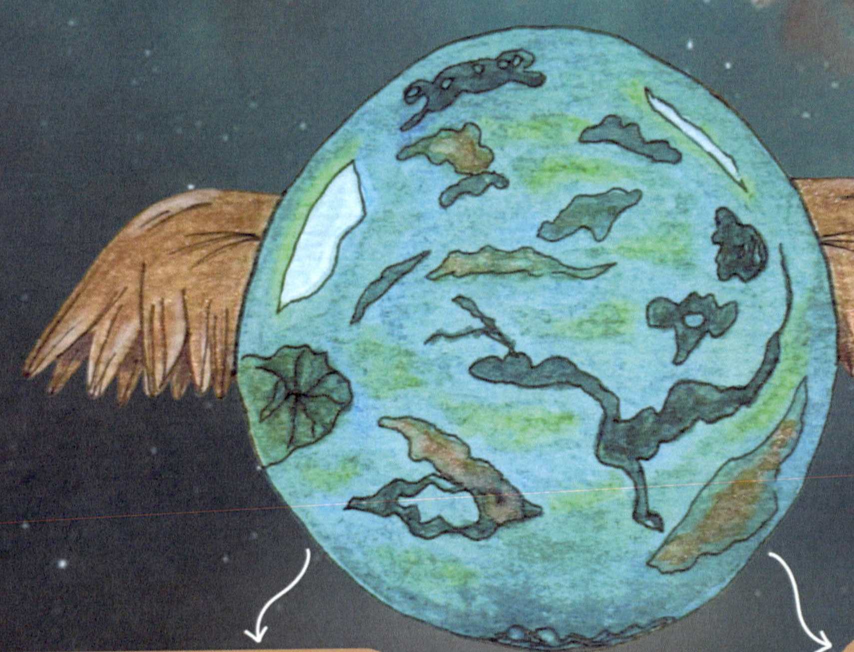

"BRING THE SPARK" - Chrys

Meet Chrysocolla, aka *Chrys*, the crystalized version of J Lo's iconic Versace dress—vibrant, unforgettable, and full of stunning blue-green energy. Infused with the powerful presence of copper, Chrys is a dynamic blend of fire and water. She's so real that some think she's fake, but this mineral spirit will encourage you to "bring the spark" to your life. That's because the copper element in Chrys' formula brings energizing qualities that stimulate your vitality, yet her magic does so in a soothing way. There's no metaphysical caffeine gitters with Chrys; she's like having a spark of inspiration sitting in your pocket that raises your confidence and fosters emotional resilience. Think of Chrys as the bridge between head and heart, guiding your words and actions from a place of genuine connection and clarity. When you need to find your authentic self and display it with confidence, grace, and a dash of style, Chrys is your go-to mineral spirit friend for transforming inner strength into outward expression.

Meet Red Agate, otherwise known as *Aggie*. They will ground your energy while inspiring confidence. With their banded, fiery colors, this mineral spirit will support your strength and resilience. Known for boosting stamina and courage, Aggie helps you face challenges with a steady, determined attitude by energizing your passions and encouraging you to take bold, confident steps forward. Whether you're tackling a challenging project or stepping way out of your comfort zone, Aggie will help you feel empowered, grounding you in the moment and fueling your motivation. While Aggie is from the mineral kingdom, if they were an animal, they would be an elephant, undeniably mighty. Carry Red Agate and let Aggie remind you that you've got "strength in every step," and all you've ever needed is and always has been inside of you.

RED AGATE *aka Aggie*

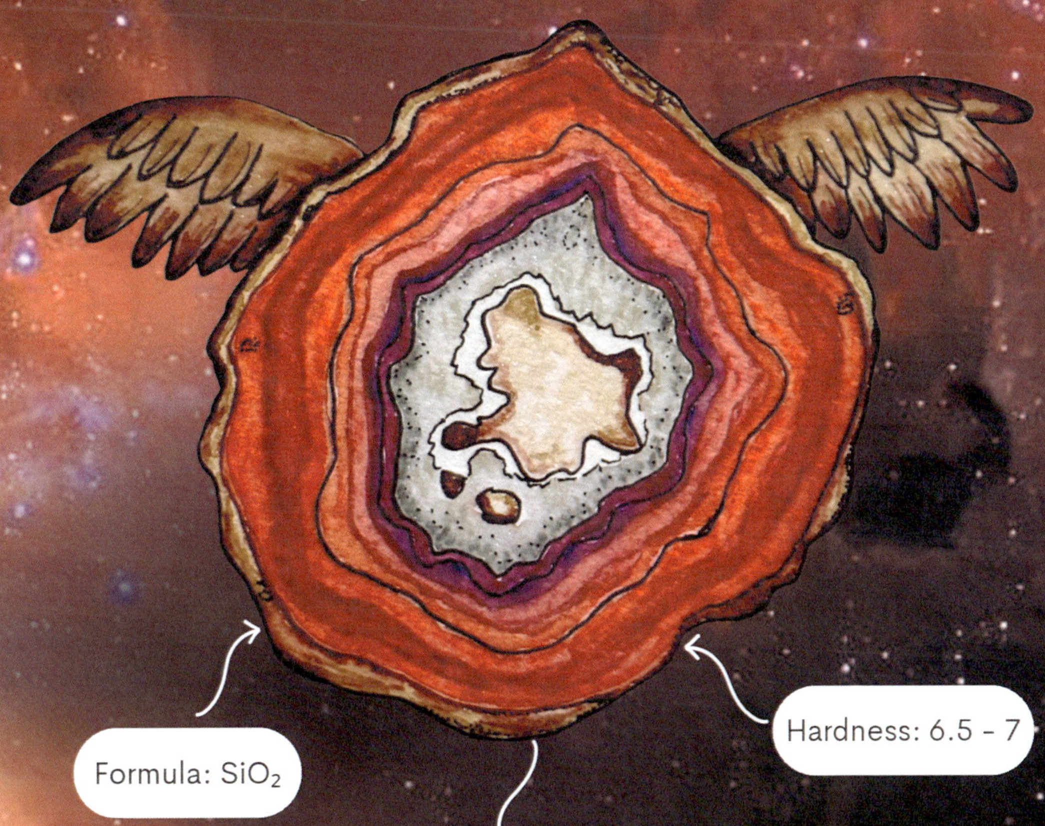

Scolecite aka Luce

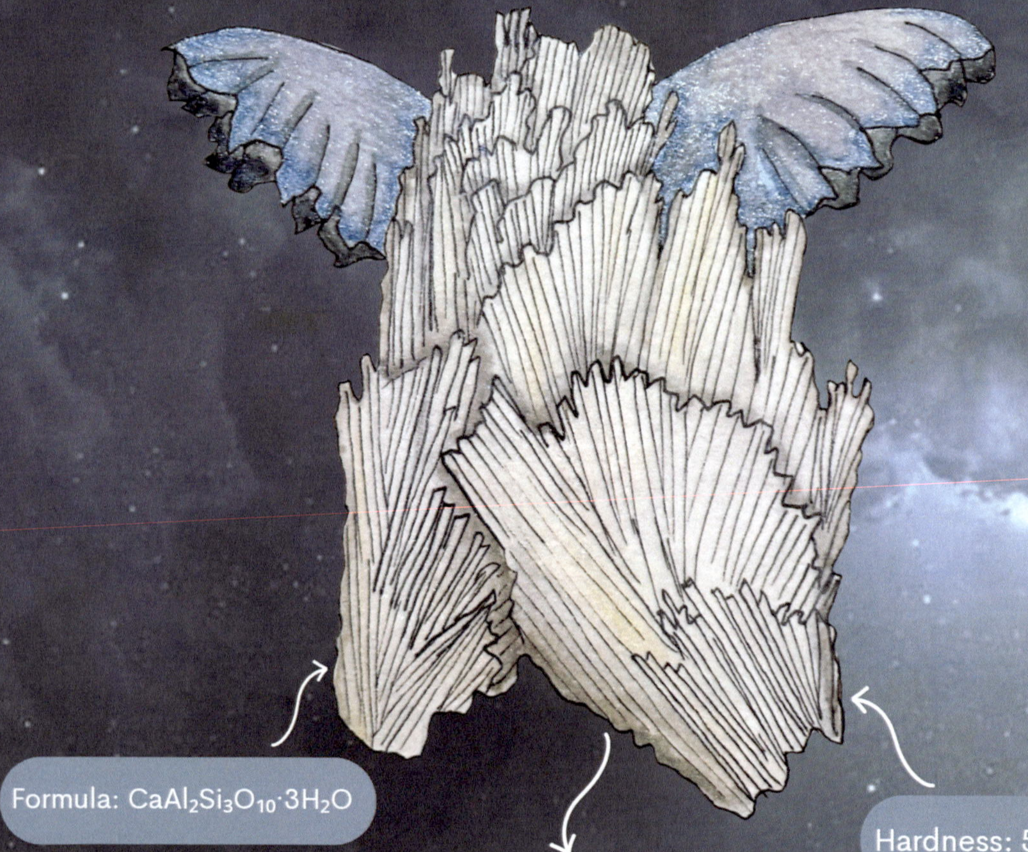

"Elevate with Ease" - Luce

Hello, Scolecite, aka "Luce," the mineral spirit that gently elevates your consciousness and cradles your spirit in a nest of cosmic fluff. Her delicate, oxymoronic needle formations rest in chubby tufts that beg to be touched. And no, Luce would not report you to HR. She's a go-to spirit pal for easing anxiety and encouraging peaceful sleep, while softly opening the door to higher awareness. Close your eyes and listen to her whispering, "Relax, breathe, and trust the process. I'm with you." Luce helps you access divine insight without the noise. Her restful energy anchors you in the present moment, creating a sacred space for spiritual growth and emotional balance. Keep Luce by your side when you're meditating because true wisdom comes from stillness. With Luce around, you'll realize that silence truly is golden.

"GET YOUR GLOW ON" - Cal

Imagine the glow of a new beginning, but all the time, and in your pocket. That's Green Calcite, aka Cal. This soothing green mineral spirit is like nature's version of a hug designed to open up your heart and foster emotional healing. Cal gently clears away emotional clutter, making space for renewal and encouraging you to embrace growth with patience and optimism. His calming energy helps dissolve the stagnation of doom scrolling, inspiring fresh ideas and renewed motivation. His presence is like hitting the reset button on your inner landscape. With his soft, seafoam-green hue, Cal reminds you that change isn't always dramatic; sometimes, it's nurturing, gentle, and beautiful. Cal is here to support your resilience and to invite abundance in love and personal transformation - gently and steadily by allowing you to, "get your glow on."

GREEN CALCITE *aka Cal*

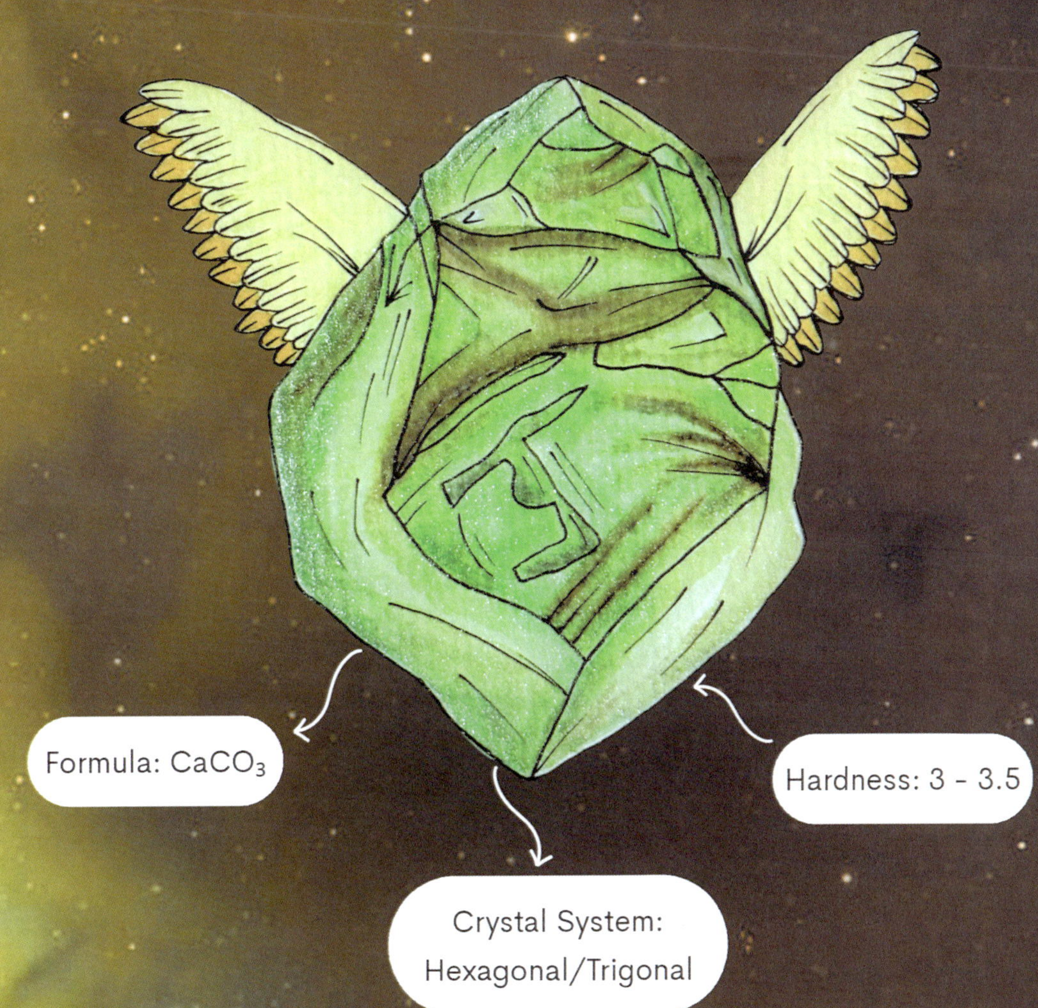

BISMUTH *aka Busy*

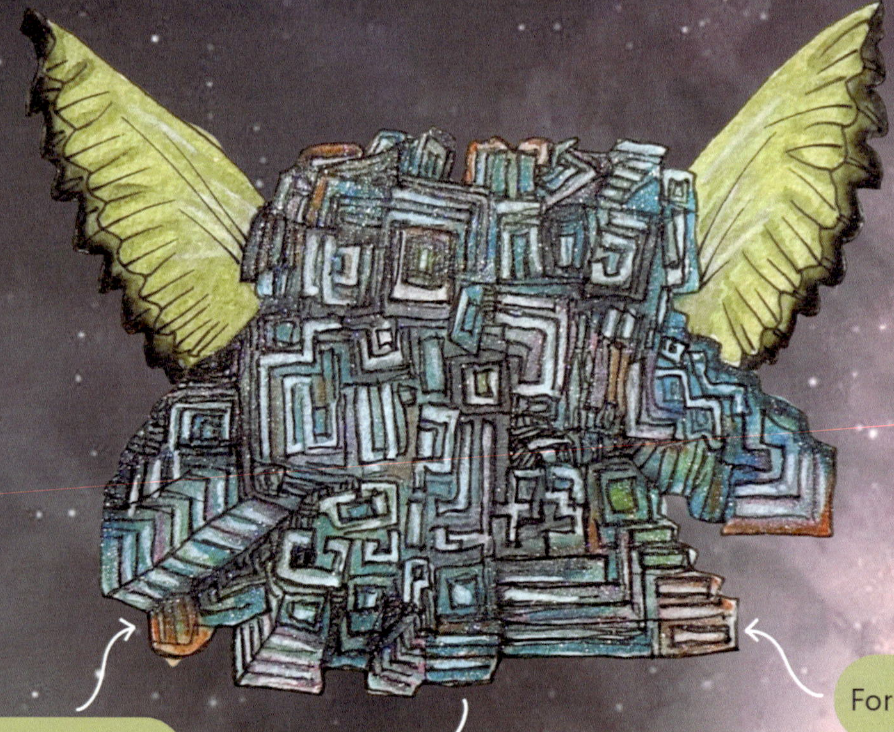

"LET YOUR REBEL SHINE" - Busy

Meet "Busy" Bismuth, the rainbow-hued rebel of the mineral world. He's like a shimmering soap bubble dancing on the edge of chaos. This fascinating guy has style and substance. He's a powerhouse for transformation and personal growth. Busy's intricate, fractal structures symbolize the beauty of complexity, reminding you that your growth journey will often take wild, unexpected turns. His vibrant, iridescent energy will activate your creativity, spark new perspectives, and help you break free from limiting beliefs. Carry Busy when you're ready to embrace change and step into your most authentic self, because sometimes, the most beautiful breakthroughs are found navigating a kaleidoscope of M.C. Escher stair-steps to the top of your own mountain summit. Busy will be your constant reminder that transformation is not linear, urging you to rebel against the status quo, celebrate the wild ride of your human experience, and shine through it.

"Listen In" - *Celine*

Meet Celestite, aka *Celine,* the sky-blue whisperer of peace and divine connection. This delicate mineral spirit inspires higher understanding. Celine will open your channels to spiritual insight and help you tune into your intuition without overwhelming your senses. She's like having a peaceful conversation with the universe; soft, clear, and reassuring. She's perfect for moments when you need to quiet your senses and invite serenity. Celine creates a calming space where you can "listen in." Her tranquil blue hues will remind you that sometimes, the most profound wisdom comes from stillness and the openness to your own divinity. After all, you are made of literal stardust - same as Celestite. Carry Celine to nurture your spiritual growth and embrace the calm confidence that comes from trusting your inner guidance. In a world that's often noisy, Celine invites you to slow down, breathe deep, and connect with the higher realms. Close your eyes. Feel your power.

Celestite *aka Celine*

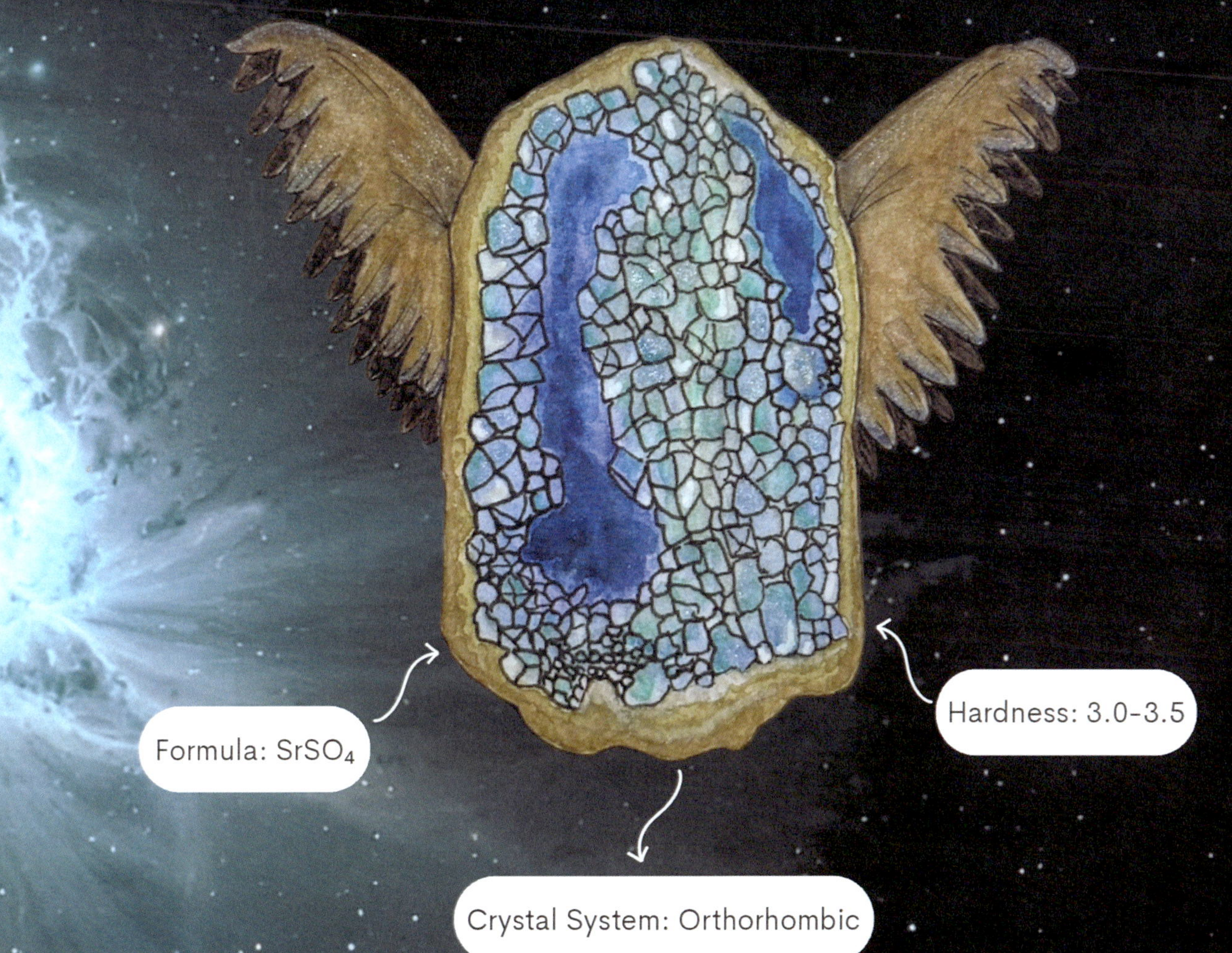

LEMURIAN QUARTZ *aka Lem*

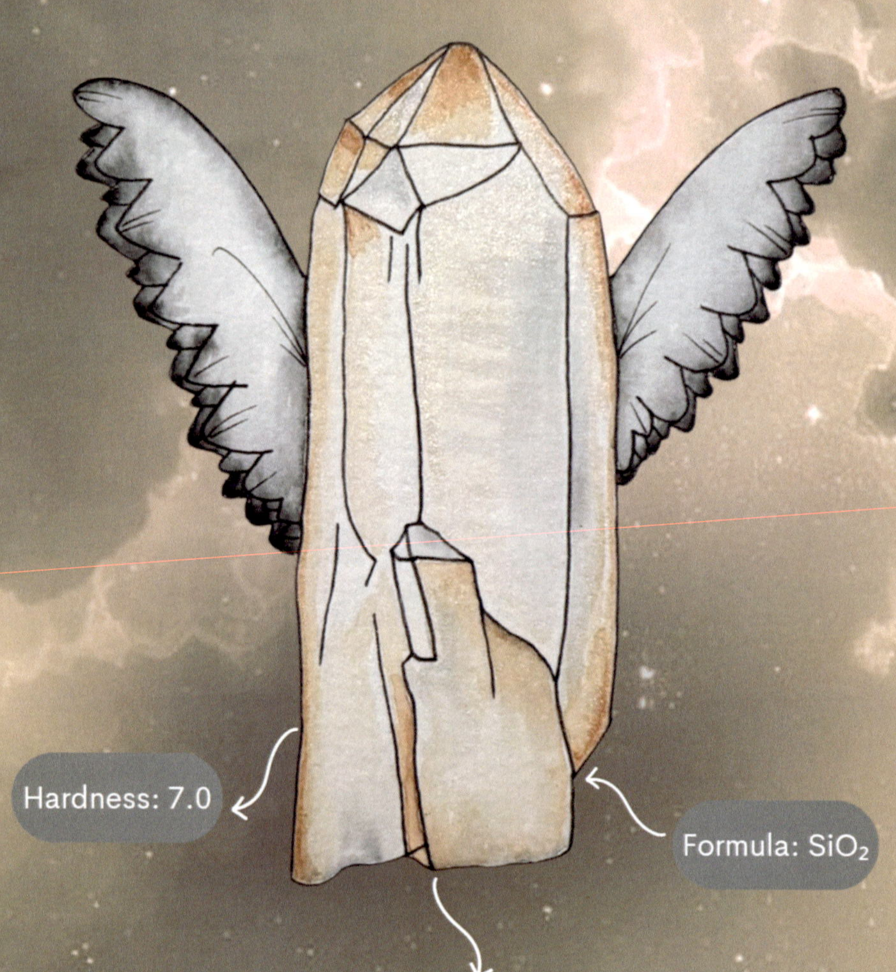

"UNLOCK HIDDEN WISDOM" - Lem

Meet Lemurian *"Lem"* Quartz, the mineral whisperer with a crystal-clear message. Known for his legendary connection to ancient wisdom, this spirit guide is like having a direct line to the universe's best advice. Lem will gently tune you into higher consciousness, helping you unlock your intuitive potential by accessing hidden insights. Think of him as your head spiritual coach. Lem's calming presence relaxes your mind and aligns your energy field, all while encouraging you to trust yourself. After all, you're one of one. With Lem at your side, you're reminded that leaning into your strengths might be the answer you seek. He is the perfect companion for deep reflection, clarity, and the embrace of your inner wisdom. Ready to level up your spiritual game? Lem will make it effortless, just like the flapping of his delicate wings.

RESOLVING HEARTBURN

What: Relationship drama with someone you genuinely love.

Who: Conscious Couple "KK" Kozi and Kai.

Why: Kozi will open your heart by clearing grudges and defensiveness, allowing you to lean into compassion and squash fire with love. Kozi will remind you that love is always the answer. She'll create space for compassion, which will enable Kai to swoop in and help you "speak your truth" from a place of pure love. His guidance will come from your limitless self, not the ego. He'll help you find the words to resolve the conflict before it boils over.

How: Place Kozi on your heart chakra and Kai on your throat chakra. Then meditate on gratitude, knowing that there is beauty in the fact that you care so dang much about someone that it hurts. Conscious Couple "KK" will come to your rescue for heartburn of the love variety.

CONSCIOUS COUPLE - KOZI & KAI

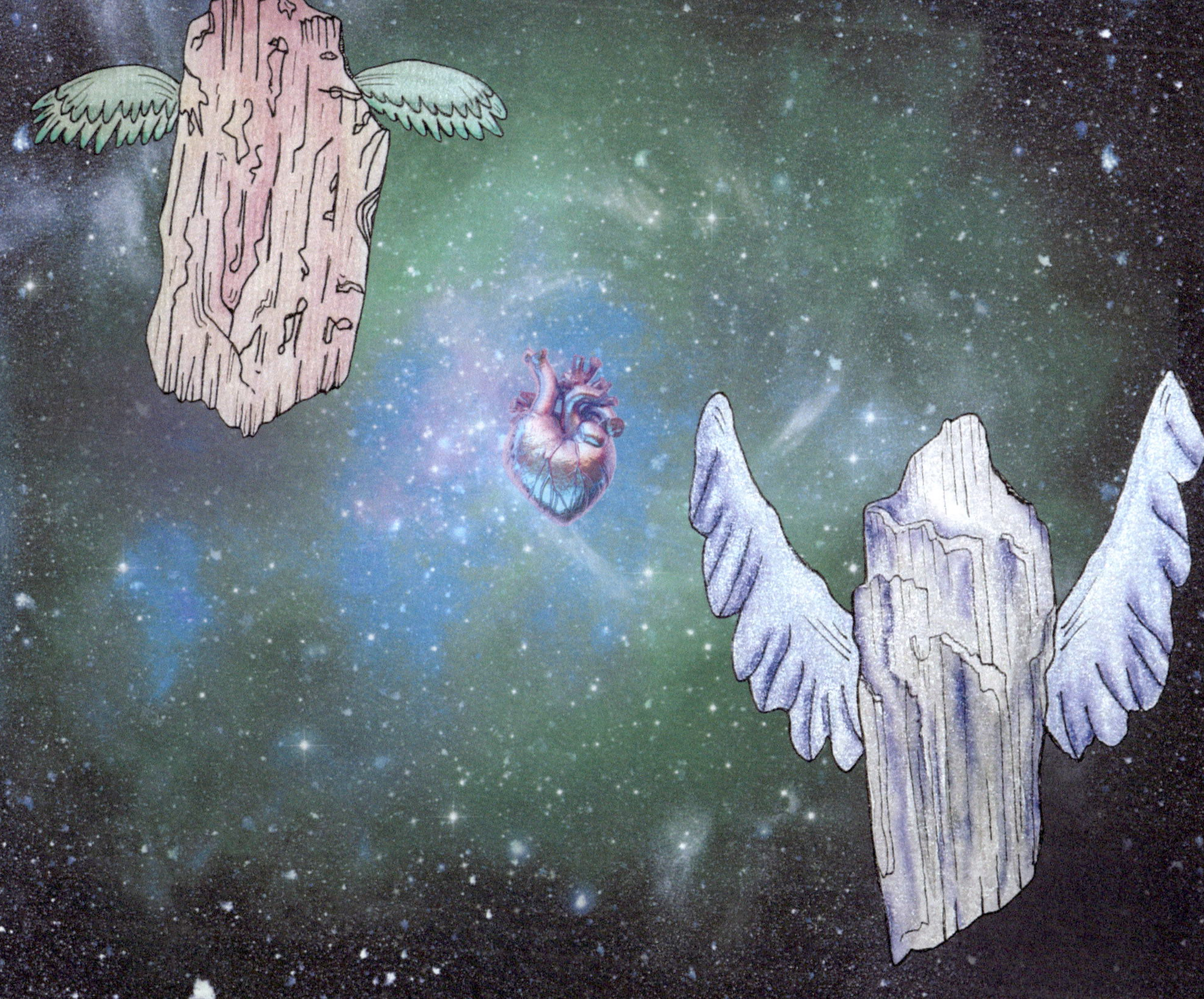

DYNAMIC DYAD - TERM & DOLLY

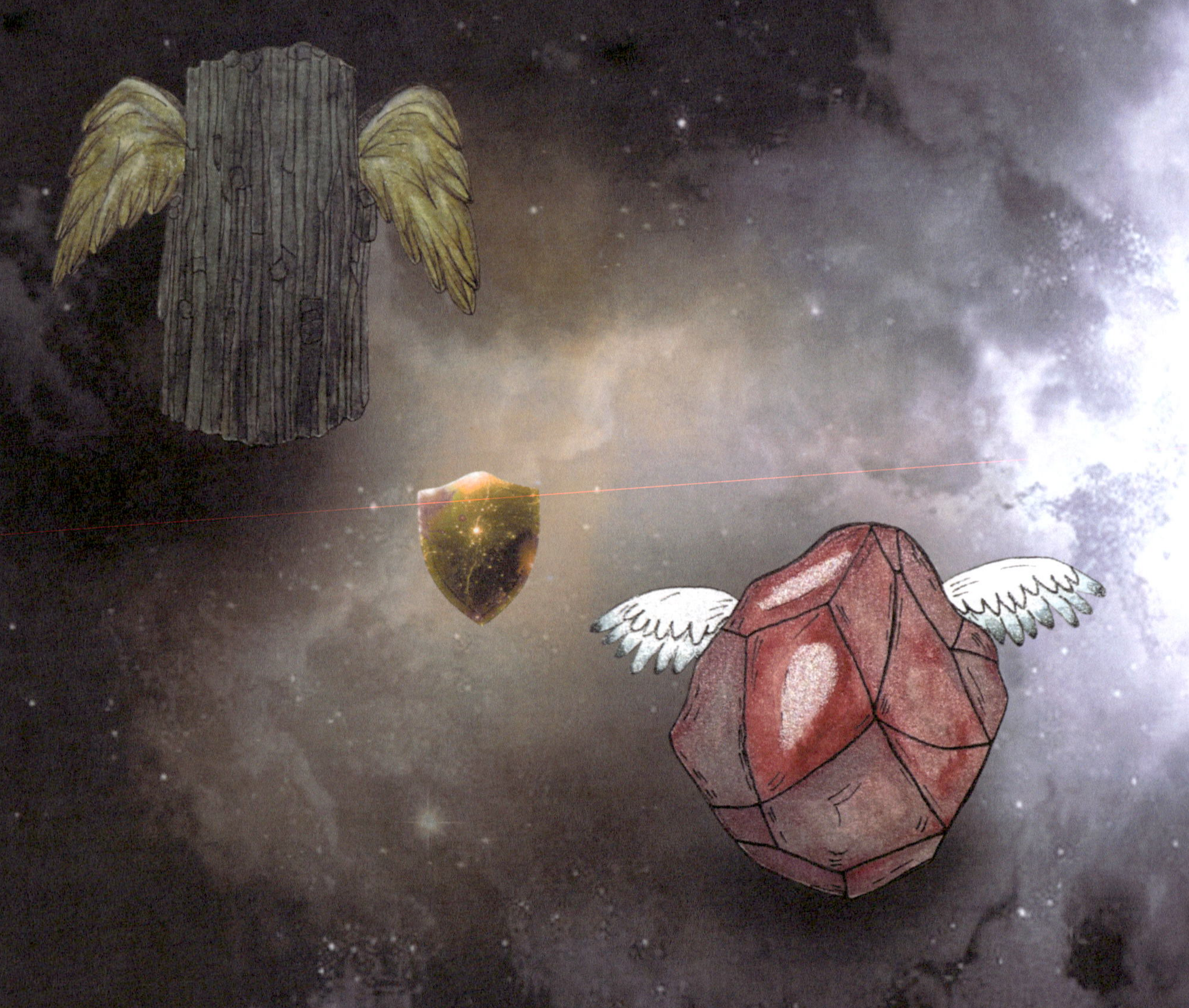

REGAIN AGENCY

What: Shift from victim mode to self-empowerment.

Who: Dynamic Dyad Term & Dolly.

Why: Feeling like you are at the effect of life happening to you is normal at times, but when the negativity of life's circumstances starts to poison your mind, you need a stronger shield and a decisive shift to regain your personal power. That's precisely what Term and Dolly will do.

How: Put Term anywhere on your person - in your pocket, in your favorite jewelry piece, or displayed on your clothing to shield you from nasty energy vampires. Wear Dolly prominently to remind you that this is YOUR life. You've won the cosmic lottery to be here. Don't let the trolls and snakes bring you down. All the power you need is inside of you. Wake up, breathe with intention, and then slay the day.

INVEST IN YOUR DREAMS

What: Taking a leap of faith and investing in your dreams.

Who: Power Pair Thistle and Mal

Why: Thistle's goal is to clear the mental clutter and bring your intuition into focus. She supports calming the mind and aligning with your purpose. Once clear of the noise, Thistle's wisdom will guide you to reveal your greater purpose. Enter Malachite Mal, the striking powerhouse ready to transform that newfound clarity into bold action. Mal encourages you to face your fears head-on, dismantling the barricades of self-doubt and paving the way for focused planning. With Mal by your side, even the most ambitious dreams become achievable goals. Together, this dynamic duo pushes you to bet on yourself.

How: Place Thistle in your meditation space to calm your mind, ignite your intuition, and focus on your life's passions. Then, hold Mal as you set your intentions, visualizing each step toward your goal. As you meditate, focus on transforming doubt into determination. Power pair Thistle & Mal assures you that the universe supports those who dare to act on their dreams. Jump, and the net will appear - that's why it's called a leap of faith.

POWER PAIR - THISTLE & MAL

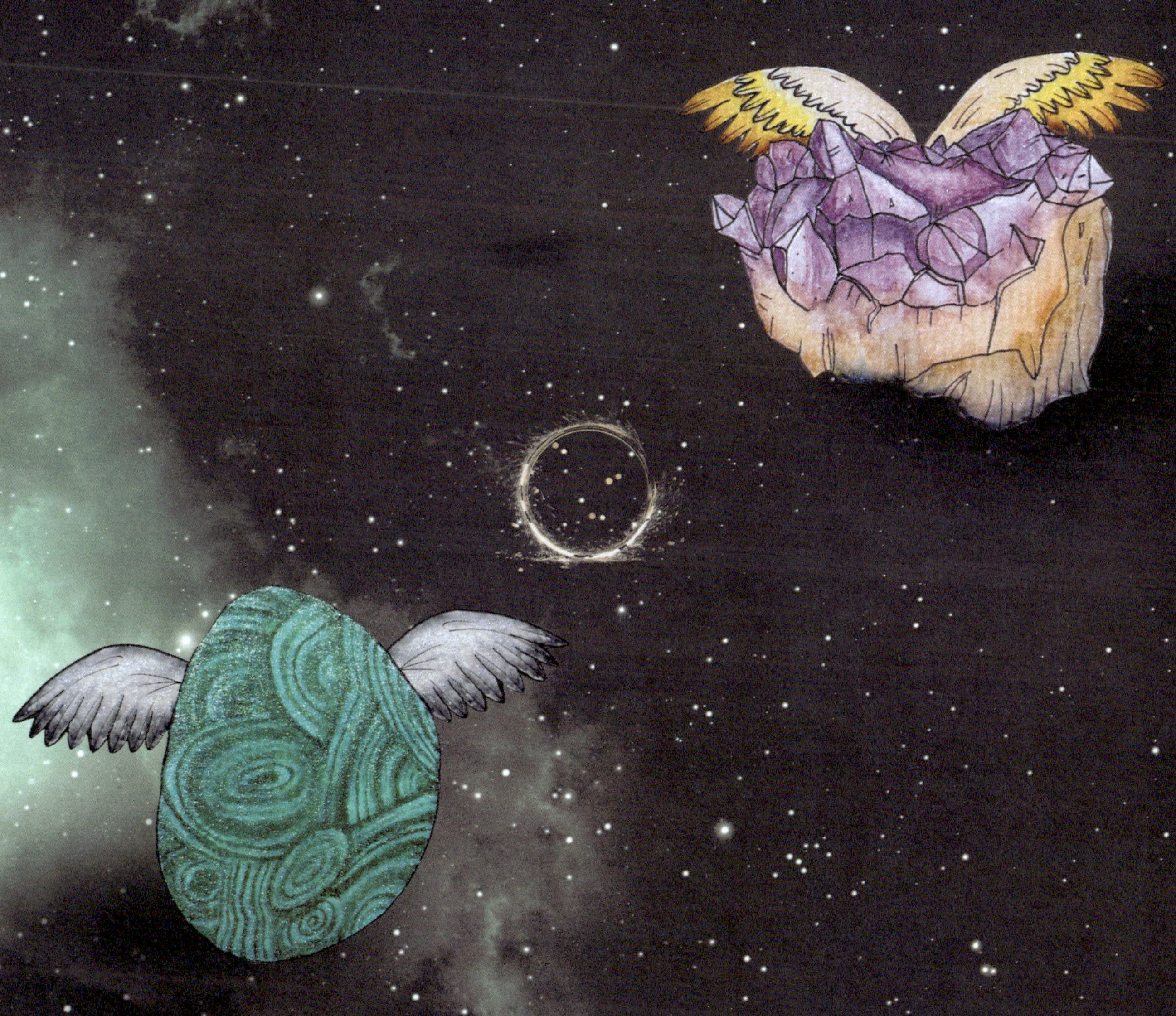

MINERAL SPIRITS VOLUME 1

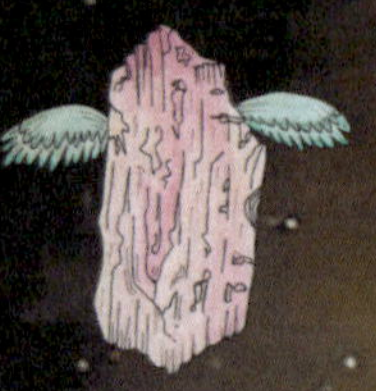

Kozi Kunzite
"Let Love Shine In"

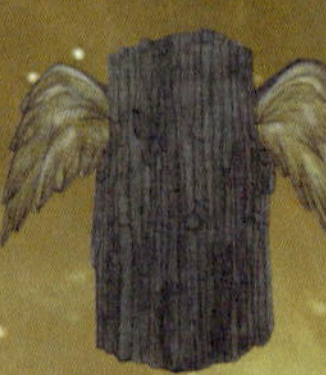

Black Tourmaline Term
"Slay Energy Vampires"

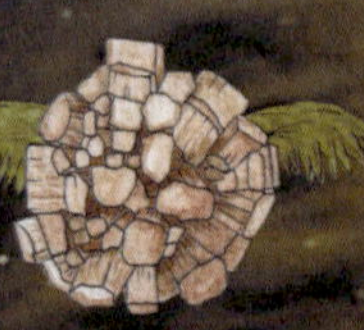

Aragonite Rag
"Round Your Edges"

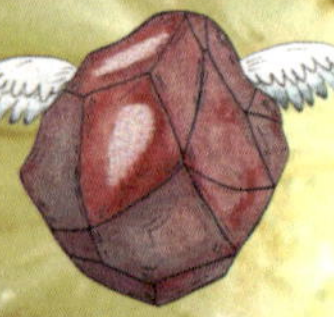

Dolly Garnet
"Ignite Your Fire"

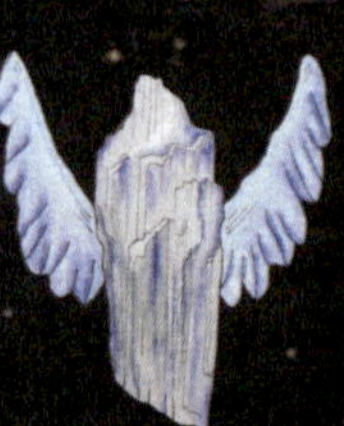

Kyanite Kai
"Speak Your Truth"

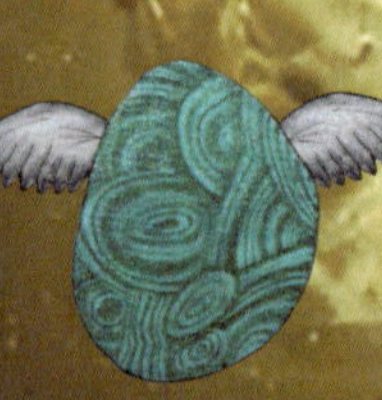

Malachite Mal
"Get Down to Business"

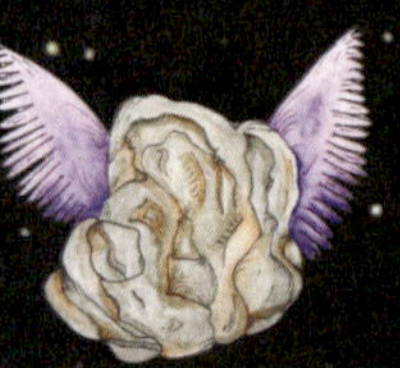

Magnesite Mags
"Quiet the Mind"

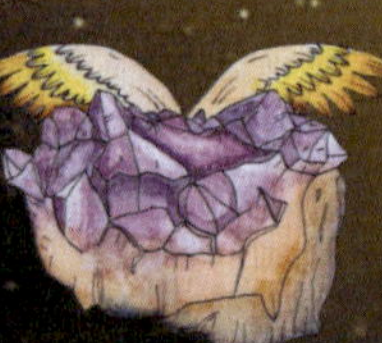

Amethyst Thistle
"Live Your Purpose"

"TRUE ESSENCE" TRIBE

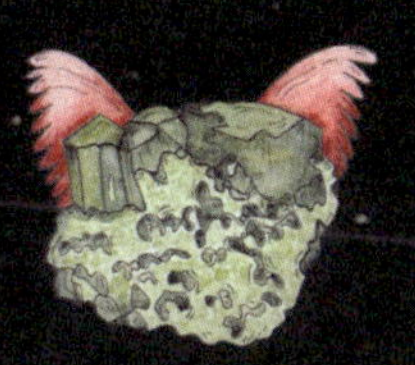

Epidote Epi
"Grow Beyond Limits"

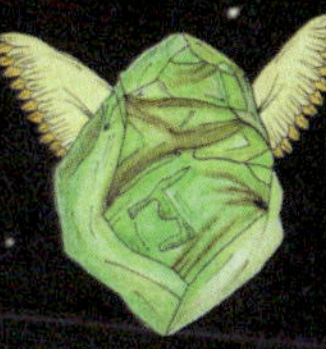

Green Calcite Cal
"Get Your Glow On"

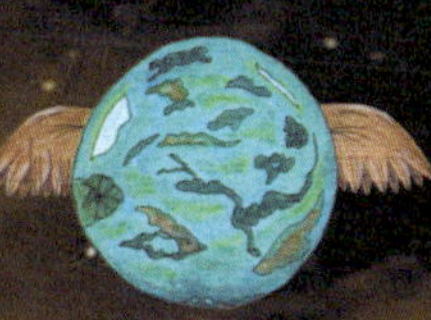

Chrysocolla Chrys
"Bring the Spark"

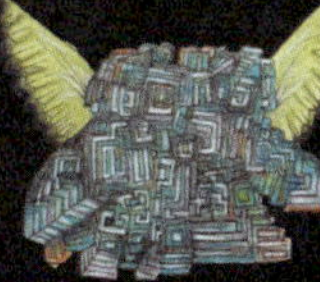

Busy Bismuth
"Let Your Rebel Shine"

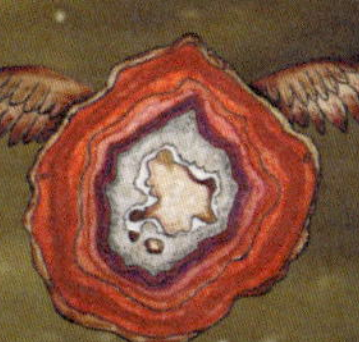

Red Agate Aggie
"Strength in Every Step"

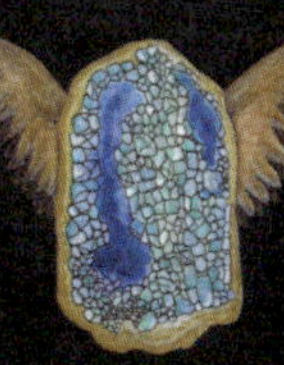

Celestite Celine
"Listen In"

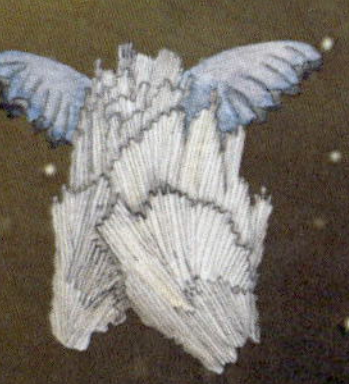

Scolecite Luce
"Elevate with Ease"

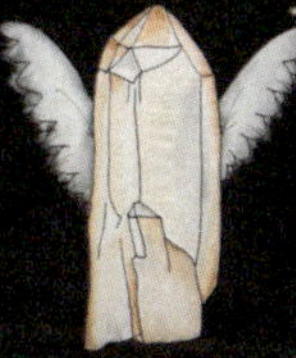

Lemurian Quartz Lem
"Unlock Hidden Wisdom"

ACKNOWLEDGEMENTS

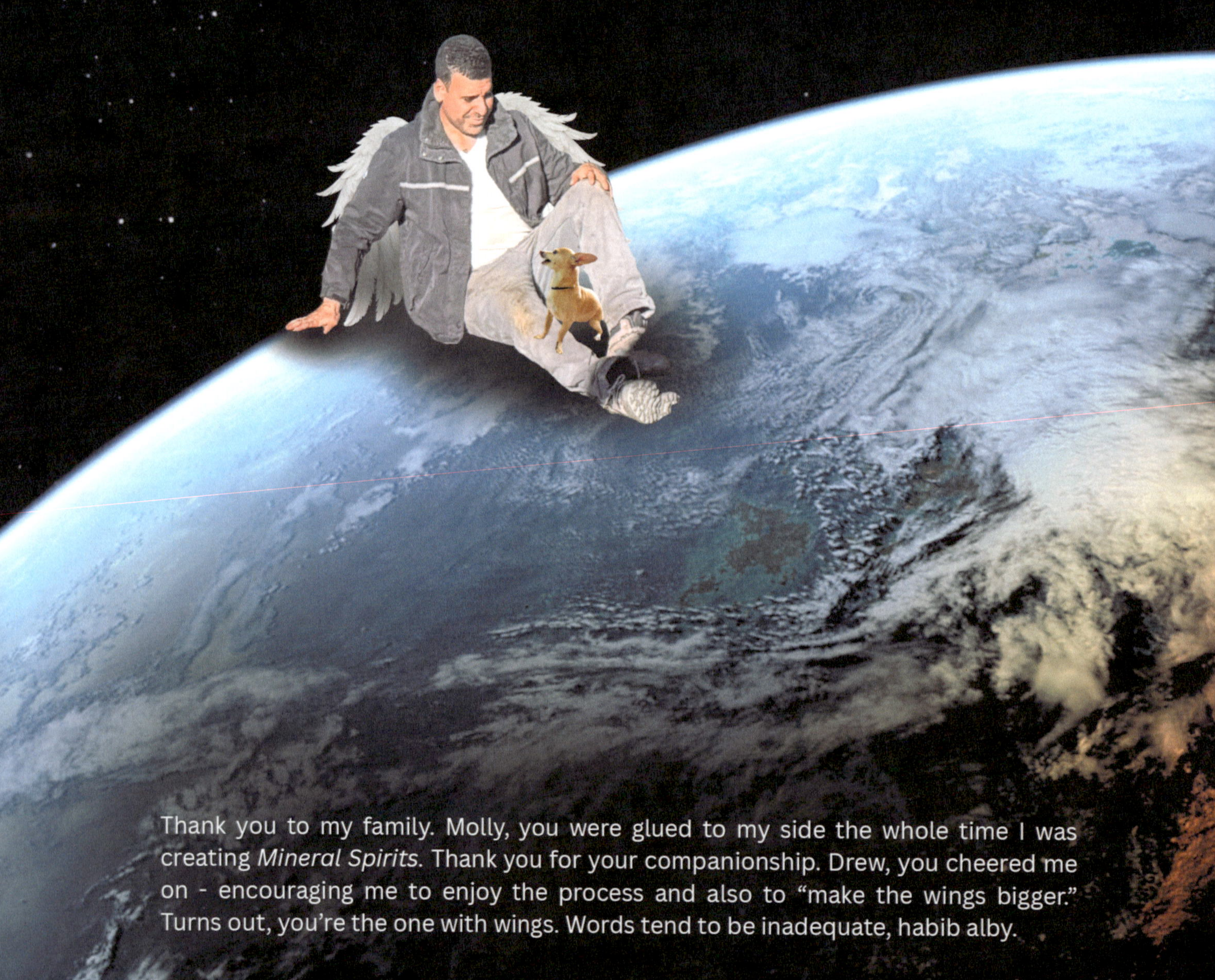

Thank you to my family. Molly, you were glued to my side the whole time I was creating *Mineral Spirits*. Thank you for your companionship. Drew, you cheered me on - encouraging me to enjoy the process and also to "make the wings bigger." Turns out, you're the one with wings. Words tend to be inadequate, habib alby.

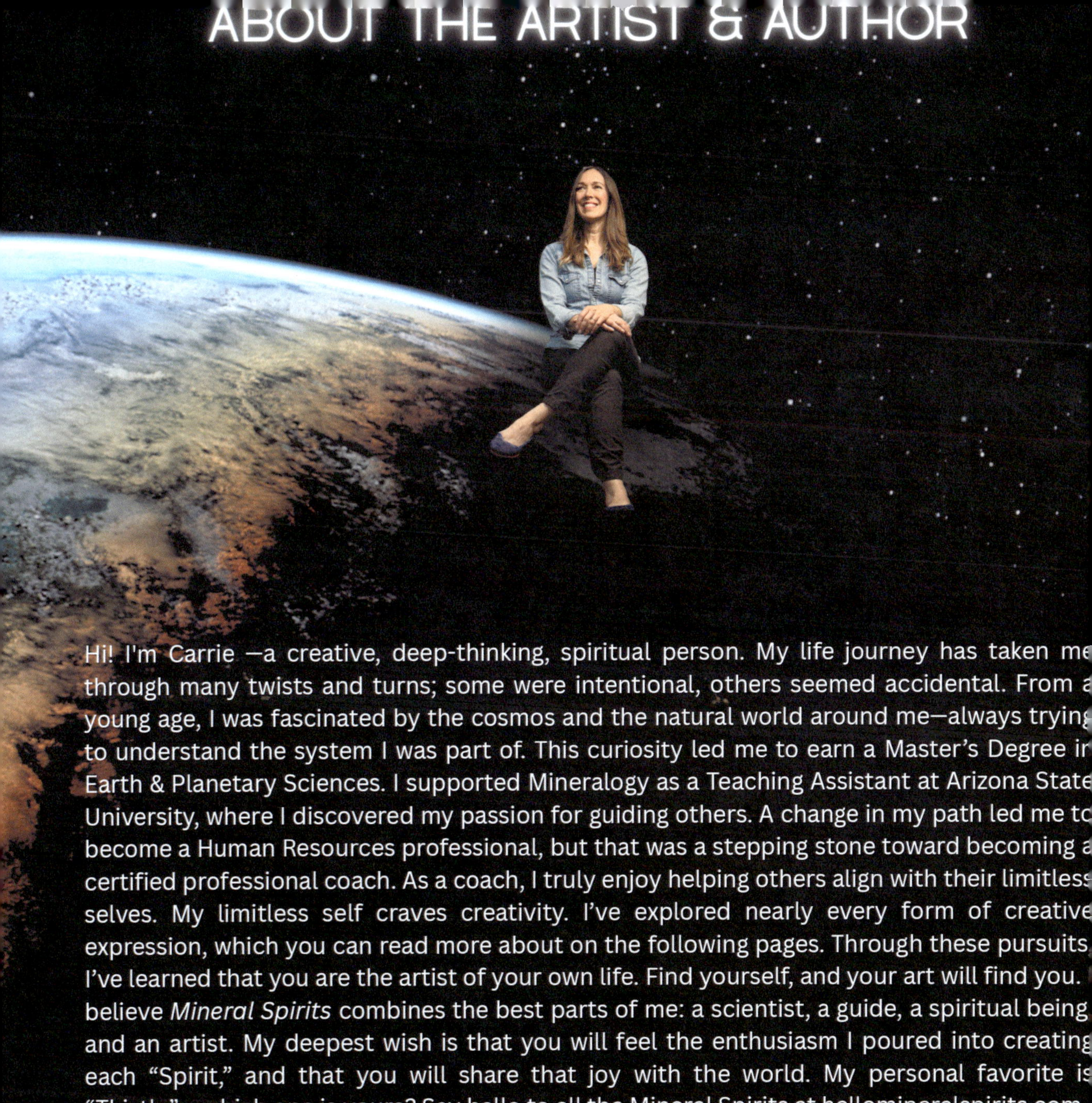

Hi! I'm Carrie —a creative, deep-thinking, spiritual person. My life journey has taken me through many twists and turns; some were intentional, others seemed accidental. From a young age, I was fascinated by the cosmos and the natural world around me—always trying to understand the system I was part of. This curiosity led me to earn a Master's Degree in Earth & Planetary Sciences. I supported Mineralogy as a Teaching Assistant at Arizona State University, where I discovered my passion for guiding others. A change in my path led me to become a Human Resources professional, but that was a stepping stone toward becoming a certified professional coach. As a coach, I truly enjoy helping others align with their limitless selves. My limitless self craves creativity. I've explored nearly every form of creative expression, which you can read more about on the following pages. Through these pursuits, I've learned that you are the artist of your own life. Find yourself, and your art will find you. I believe *Mineral Spirits* combines the best parts of me: a scientist, a guide, a spiritual being, and an artist. My deepest wish is that you will feel the enthusiasm I poured into creating each "Spirit," and that you will share that joy with the world. My personal favorite is "Thistle" —which one is yours? Say hello to all the Mineral Spirits at hellomineralspirits.com.

THE PATH TO MAKING MINERAL SPIRITS

1980's Illinois: Summer paper making class

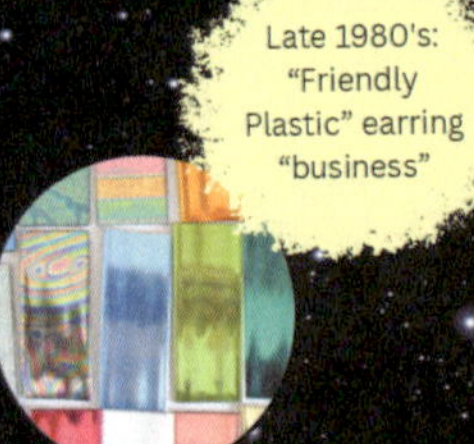

Late 1980's: "Friendly Plastic" earring "business"

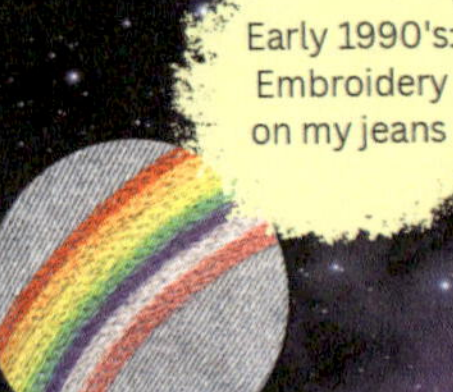

Early 1990's: Embroidery on my jeans

Childhood piano and high school choir

Mid 1990's: Poetry wins 2nd place in contest

Late 1990's: Photography and Yearbook Layout camp

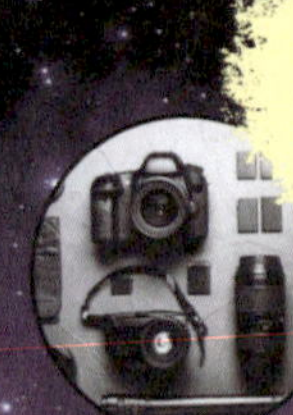

2006 Denver: Large acrylic canvas paintings

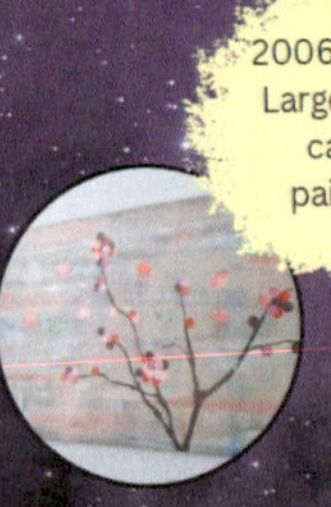

2008 Denver: Screenwriting class

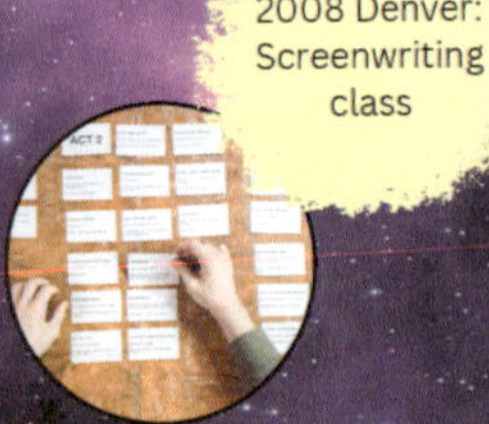

2015 NYC: Acting classes

2019 NJ: Acrylic on canvas and terrarium mobile

2019 NJ: Holiday ornament making with Drew

COVID-19 Woodworking

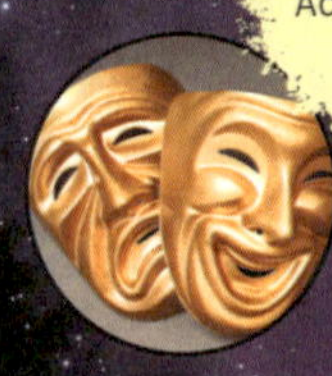

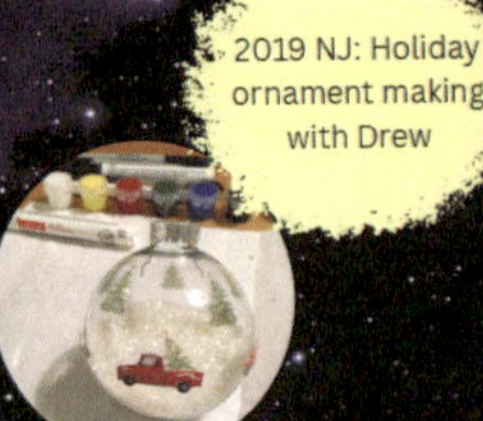

"FIND YOURSELF AND YOUR ART WILL FIND YOU"

2020 NJ Scrapbooking and 1st YouTube

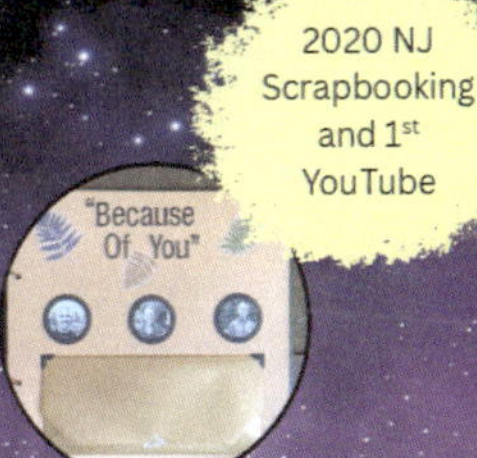

2020 NJ Watercolor New Moon notecards

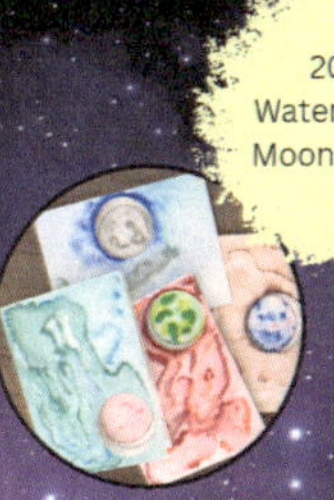

2021 CA: Interior design and macrame

2021 CA: Lathe woodworking

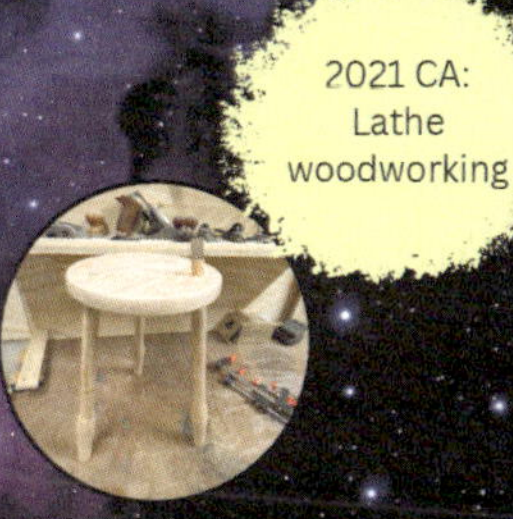

2022 CA: Furniture restoration & YouTube channel

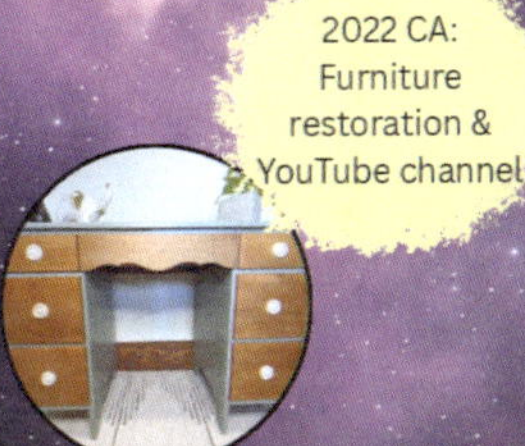

2022 CA: 1st Self-published career book

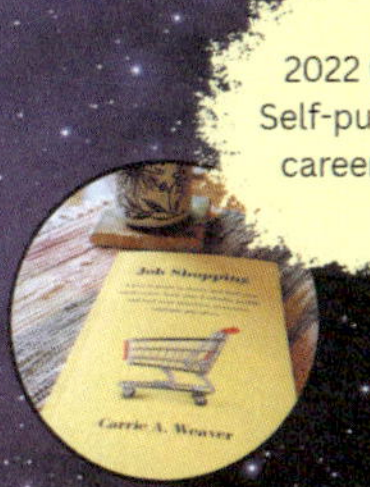

2023 CA: Stained glass making

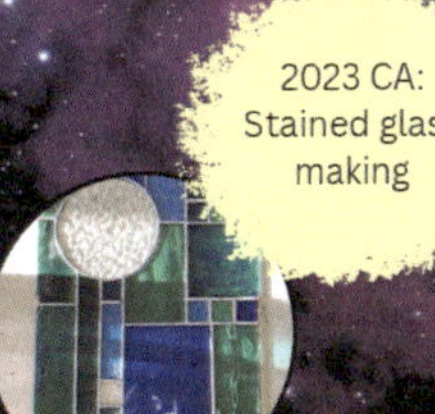

2024 UC Berkeley Interior Architecture model making

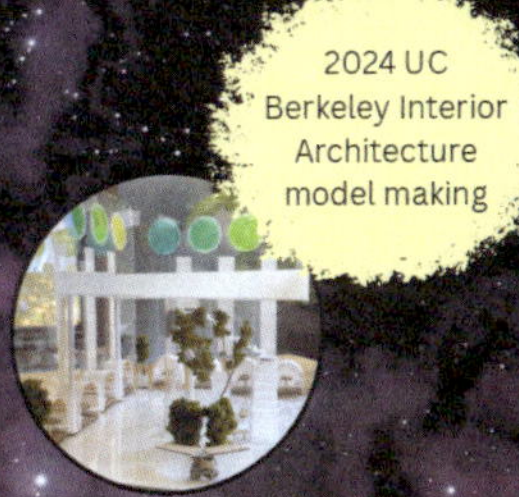

2024 UC Berkeley Color Theory class painting

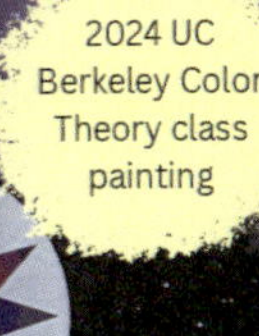

2024 UC Berkeley Design Communication pencil drawing

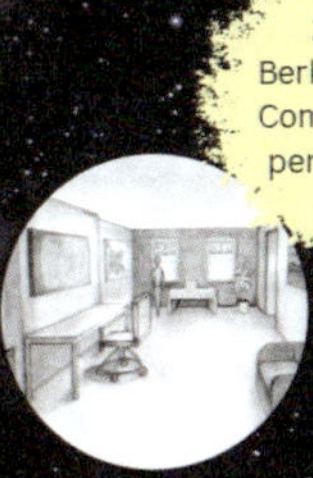

2025 Watercolor ego vs. limitless self visualization

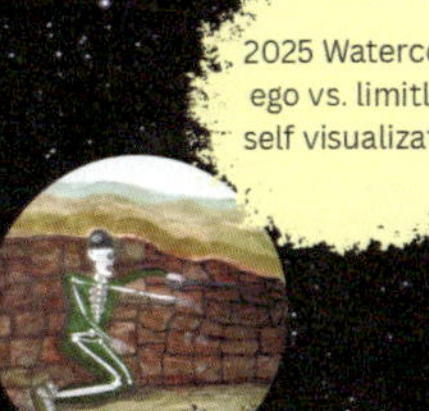

Oct 2025: 1st Mineral Spirit is born

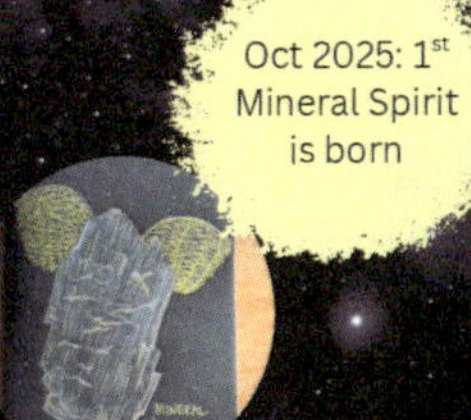

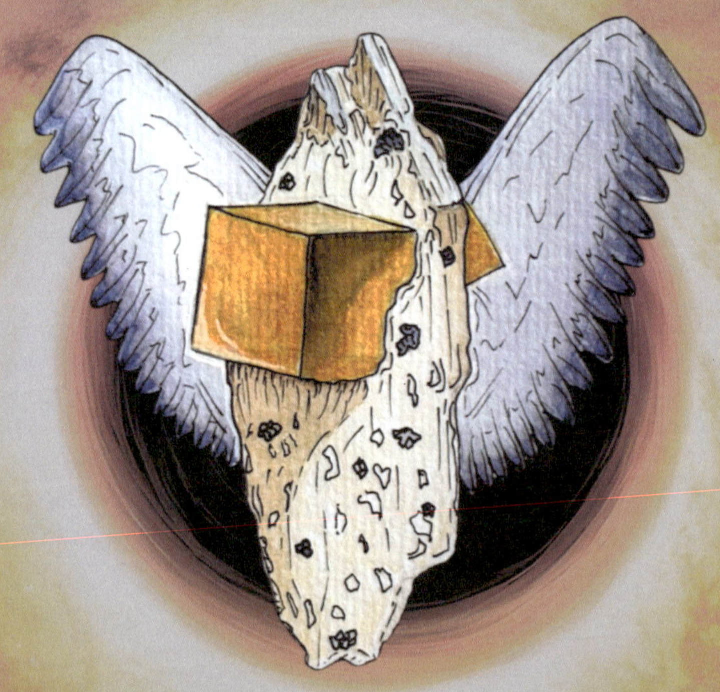

Meet **pyrite** *aka* Pye

www.ingramcontent.com/pod-product-compliance
Lightning Source LLC
Chambersburg PA
CBRC092052150726
48005CB00031B/1024